Praise for Barbara Marx Hubbard

"There is no doubt in my mind that Barbara Marx Hubbard, who helped introduce the concept of futurism to society, is the best informed human now alive regarding futurism and the foresights it has produced."
— R. BUCKMINSTER FULLER, inventor and social architect

"If I have ever met a person who is fully conscious of her responsibilities toward the earth, humanity, and the cosmos, it is certainly Barbara Marx Hubbard. She is a true twenty-first-century woman."
— ROBERT MULLER, former United Nations assistant secretary general

"Renowned as a futurist, Barbara Marx Hubbard also plants her feet firmly in today. In fact, her wit and wisdom always seem to be saying, 'The best way to get anywhere is to start from where you are.' I am grateful for the many things I have learned from her."
— GENE RODDENBERRY, creator of *Star Trek*

"Barbara Marx Hubbard is a true visionary, demonstrating by her words and actions her commitment to a sustainable future."
— JOHN DENVER, singer/songwriter

Praise for *Conscious Evolution*

"*Conscious Evolution* is an essential book. I recommend it enthusiastically."
— GARY ZUKAV, author of *The Seat of the Soul*

"[Barbara Marx Hubbard] has done an invaluable service in *Conscious Evolution* by clarifying the urgent issues, summarizing much of the notable literature that pertains to a global renaissance, compiling a practical resource guide, and sounding the call that will ignite us all to become cocreators. This is a wonderful and important book."
CE OF MIND

T0162939

CONSCIOUS EVOLUTION

CONSCIOUS EVOLUTION

Awakening the Power
of Our Social Potential

REVISED EDITION

Barbara Marx Hubbard

New World Library
Novato, California

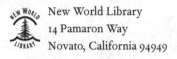 New World Library
14 Pamaron Way
Novato, California 94949

Text design by Tona Pearce Myers
Illustration inside front cover by Teresa Collins

Library of Congress Cataloging-in-Publication Data
Hubbard, Barbara Marx, date.
Conscious evolution : awakening the power of our social potential / Barbara Marx Hubbard ; foreword to the revised edition by Terry Patten ; foreword by Neale Donald Walsch. — Revised edition.
    pages   cm
ISBN 978-1-60868-117-4 (paperback) — ISBN 978-1-60868-118-1 (ebook)
1. Social evolution. 2. Social ethics. 3. Social ecology. 4. Social participation.
I. Title.
HM626.H83 2015
302'.14—dc23   2014042455

First printing of revised edition, February 2015
ISBN 978-1-60868-117-4
Printed in Canada

 New World Library is proud to be a Gold Certified Environmentally Responsible Publisher. Publisher certification awarded by Green Press Initiative. www.greenpressinitiative.org

10 9 8 7 6 5 4 3 2

*Dedicated to all pioneering souls on Earth
who are awakening and participating in a gentle birth
of the new era of human evolution*

Contents

PART I. THE NEW STORY OF CREATION

PART II. CONSCIOUS EVOLUTION: A NEW WORLDVIEW

PART III. THE SOCIAL POTENTIAL MOVEMENT

PART IV. THE GREAT AWAKENING

Acknowledgments

I wish to acknowledge people who have been an inspiration and loves of my life.

I honor my partner Sidney Lanier, Episcopal priest and artistic theater producer, who made his transition in 2013. He came and found me when I was not sure of my direction and said, "Barbara, it's *conscious evolution*!" We founded the Foundation for Conscious Evolution together in 1993 with a grant from Laurance Rockefeller to bring forth the vision of humanity's conscious evolution. I would like to quote here a paragraph from his book *The Sovereign Person: A Soul's Call to Conscious Evolution*:

> The universe is in us. We are the fruit of the vine called "terra mater," endeavoring to interiorize an intense focus of intelligence and intuitive feeling into a radiant cosmic person, a sentient microcosm that from its felt unity can germinate into an infinite series of differential manifestations transforming Matter into dynamic energy to create a galactic civilization from our planetary culture.[1]

I thank my five children: Suzanne, Woodleigh, Alexandra, Lloyd, and Wade. My son Wade has passed but is much beloved. My children, my eight grandchildren, and I have built a family clan and a shared "trajectory" toward our conscious evolution, through life purpose, each in our own way, and for this I am grateful. I thank my eldest daughter, Suzanne, my partner in all our work and a pioneer in the discovery of the nature of the universal human and the application of conscious evolution in the daily lives of people everywhere.

I thank Patricia Gaul, executive director of the Foundation for Conscious Evolution, and her husband, Norman Kremer, who have helped to spread the message of conscious evolution, growing the foundation into a worldwide organization for the past fifteen years. I thank Lucky Sweeney for stepping in to repattern the foundation, and Jane Johnson for her exceptional social media and organizationally supportive contributions. And Teresa Collins and Marshall Lefferts, who first pioneered with me the way to use the internet to "tell the new story" of conscious evolution, as the first directors of the Foundation for Conscious Evolution.

I have special gratitude to Stephen Dinan, CEO of The Shift Network, who brought my teachings on conscious evolution to the internet, where they now reach many thousands of students. Stephen also was the producer of the first Planetary Birth Celebration, on December 22, 2012, fulfilling a profound dream of my life: that we announce to the world that something new is being born through us. He is a partner in the great calling of healing and evolving our world.

I want to thank all the members of the board of the Foundation for Conscious Evolution; my sister Patricia Ellsberg, teacher of the Emergence Process and partner in all my work; and Sister Judy Cauley, a cocreator who connected me with thousands of Catholic sisters and evolutionary leaders in the Church and the world. Thanks to Carolyn Anderson, coauthor of *The Co-Creator's Handbook* and coeditor of *52 Codes for Conscious Self Evolution*, who managed my vice-presidential campaign; to Katharine and Makasha Roske, founders of the Hummingbird Community, the first community based on conscious evolution and the practices of cocreation; and Joanne Brem, dearest guide and business coach. I thank Barbara Fields, director of the Association for Global New Thought, a prime companion and guide through so many projects; Darrell Laham, brilliant creator of the first model design for the Synergy Engine, vital to the Peace Room; Claudia Welss, my first PhD student and my friend; and Sandra de Castro Buffington, magnificent pioneer who brings innovative media to the world. Also, John Zwerver, who made his transition in 2013, for his presidency of the foundation and his tireless work on its behalf; Rinaldo Brutoco, head of the World Business Academy, our business adviser and dear friend; Avon Mattison, my partner in developing the Wheel of Cocreation and bringing it into practice in the world through the United Nations and other peace organizations worldwide; and to my dear friend Eve Konstanine, as well as Anne Milgrim, who has been a pillar of strength.

I want to love and honor my deceased husband, Earl Hubbard, artist and philosopher, with whom I began the search for the "new story" and the worldview of conscious evolution.

Special gratitude to Lt. Col. John J. Whiteside, who founded with me the Committee for the Future and produced the twenty-five SYNCON conferences that inspired me to run for vice president of the United States on the Democratic ticket.

So many colleagues have inspired me in my love of conscious evolution as the optimum worldview for the fulfillment of our potential. They include Teilhard de Chardin; Sri Aurobindo and the Mother; Buckminster Fuller, who guided me in the Design

Science Revolution; and Dr. Abraham Maslow, who inspired me to become "self-actualizing." Dr. Jonas Salk revealed to me the nature of the evolutionary human, and Jean Houston and Hazel Henderson were the first evolutionary women who woke me up to my own feminine power. To Neale Donald Walsch, dear friend, who guided me in telling the story through his remarkable biography of me: *The Mother of Invention.* To my agent, Bill Gladstone, a tireless advocate of conscious evolution. I thank Ervin Laszlo, Terry Patten, Jerome Glenn, A. Harris (Bud) Stone, Duane Elgin, Peter Russell, Craig Hamilton, Diane Williams, Debra Moldow, and all the Evolutionary Leaders.

I also thank Marc Allen, publisher of New World Library, who had so much faith in these new ideas and urged me to write this book and more to come.

In a special category, I wish to acknowledge the extraordinary input of my friend and colleague Mark Donohue. He spent hundreds of hours with me helping to bring the vision into greater clarity and pragmatic usefulness. His assistance was of incomparable value. As a socially responsible businessman, he understands how to apply conscious evolution to the practical purpose of evolving capitalism itself. He can be an important communicator and developer of this work in the world.

Foreword to the Revised Edition

What if evolution, after unfolding *unconsciously* for billions of years, is now in the process of becoming *self-aware*, and for the first time intentionally *choosing* its future expressions?

It is impossible to overstate the power of this simple big idea.

Evolution has a 13.8-billion-year history. Many universities are now telling the story of "Big History." They see a single thread running through evolution — connecting the billions of years after the big bang, in which the physical cosmos and solar system evolved, with the hundreds of millions of years of biological evolution on Earth, and now with the tens of thousands of years of human cultural evolution, which we now see shaping the future of millions of species and ecosystems.

Darwin's theory of natural selection hypothesizes that the trajectory of evolution has been a by-product of the churning chaos of countless apparently random events, local choices, and unaccountable emergences. Apes never decided to evolve into humans. They evolved into humans because certain apes had biological adaptations that made them more fit for survival; thus, their genes and offspring survived. Over time, these adaptations caused the whole species to evolve from apes into humans. In this theory, conscious choice has not played a role in guiding any step of the evolutionary process.

This book unabashedly *advocates* for the significance of conscious evolution. As Barbara Marx Hubbard makes abundantly clear, *we are now the eyes of evolution*. Humans now know that our choices have evolutionary implications. With that, everything has changed. An evolutionary phase change is upon us.

This idea opens the door to many other hugely important questions. Some of the most compelling bring it to a very personal level:

- Does conscious evolution imply the intentional participation of individuals? What does effective individual participation entail?
- If you take it seriously, what does conscious evolution mean to the individual? Is it a creative opportunity? A moral obligation? An existential challenge?
- What does it mean to the relationships among individuals who feel called to participate?

It frames our most serious concerns:

- Since the evolutionary process (of which we are a part) wants to keep evolving, how can we make the choices necessary to avert impending disasters that might bring serious evolutionary regression?
- How will intelligent choices find a timely way into political and economic implementation?

It also invites us to think courageously and expansively:

- What glorious and heretofore unimaginable possibilities might be opened up by conscious evolution?
- What potentials might evolution, in order to keep evolving, *not* choose? And how can such conservative choices be healthily enacted? How will evolution mediate competing values?
- How will awareness alter the very nature of evolutionary change?

None of these questions were even imagined in 1963 when Barbara Marx Hubbard made it her business to initiate the process that led her to imagining them.

The idea of conscious evolution is what catalyzed, in the mid-1960s, a powerful experience of expanded reality in a young woman who was then a Connecticut housewife and mother of five. Barbara Marx Hubbard had recently become inspired after reading Teilhard de Chardin, Buckminster Fuller, and Sri Aurobindo Ghose.

Within just a few years, she was on the board of the World Future Society, living in the nation's capital. Although her inner life had become that of a (rational) mystic of the future, she was hanging out with leading scientists and behaving like an impassioned activist. She called herself a "futurist." In the process she was catalyzing innovative conversations among many remarkable men and women, including Jonas Salk, Buckminster Fuller, Abraham Maslow, and NASA scientists.

This simple idea quickly took over her life. But for her it wasn't "just" an idea; it was a consuming, deep, personal relationship with the spirit of evolutionary emergence. It took almost thirty-five more years for her to write *Conscious Evolution*.

In those years, Barbara convened a series of large-scale

catalytic meetings. She befriended leading thinkers all over the world. In 1984 she ran for vice president of the United States and, in an occasion of nonordinary reality, her name was put into formal nomination for the vice presidency at the Democratic Convention held that year in San Francisco (the same convention at which Geraldine Ferraro became the first woman to receive a major political party's nomination). She wrote four books before 1998.

But these outer activities were just half the story. Her inner life was only intensifying. She read voraciously and dialogued with thought leaders and ordinary citizens. In the process, she contributed many key ideas to the evolving edge of culture.

Perhaps my favorite example is her insight that on any planet, if an intelligent species evolved it would eventually succeed to a degree that would overpopulate the planet, damage companion species, and choke the species on its own waste. "Our crisis is a birth," she often points out. It is a *natural process*, one that will open into a birth of the next, more universal version of the human species.

Her insights are rational, logical, and informed by the scientific worldview. However, they are also bright, optimistic, fresh, playful, and full of the very force of life — a youthful spirit that she continues to communicate vividly even at eighty-four years of age.

Early in this process Barbara began to wake up before dawn to contemplate the intelligence of evolution and to enter into communion with it. She would sometimes receive electrifying "downloads" from that spirit of emergence, some of which have gone on to have enormous cultural impact.

Thus, for most of her life Barbara has lived in two worlds. On one hand, her natural language has been that of evolution and futurism and science and rationality. On the other hand, she has been having profound and empowering mystical experiences of a consciousness and presence that she understood as the "Christ presence." Even though her mystical communion was often with the spirit of evolutionary emergence, she had experiences of initiation and activation that are better understood in mystical circles than scientific ones. She discovered that her two feet were firmly and irrevocably planted in two apparently incommensurate and nonintersecting worlds. It took her a while to become fully comfortable in her skin and able to communicate her message.

Thus, by the time she was ready to write *Conscious Evolution* in 1997, she had tested and refined the ideas and the vision it expresses during three decades of research, study, teaching, and activism. She had integrated her scientific evolutionary thinking with her mystical soul and spirit. This book communicates a developed expression of this all-important idea of conscious evolution, as well as the accompanying key idea — that our crisis is a natural process leading to a birth.

It also begins to communicate what has since become the thrust of her work — mentoring other mystics of the future in the experiential journey of becoming conscious evolutionaries. She invites the reader into her vision of possibility, bringing forward her fierce, "telerotic" spirit of playfulness, faith, optimism, commitment, and seductive invitation. In the seventeen years since this volume was published, it has inspired hundreds of thousands of men and women all over the world and helped spark the growing movement of evolutionaries with a calling to serve the world in evolving toward greater consciousness and freedom. Because this text has been a source of inspiration and guidance to so many other pioneering souls, it resonates with extra power, making it even more valuable to anyone engaged in or beginning his or her unique version of the inner and outer journey Barbara has traversed.

So, enjoy! Seventeen years later, this classic is even more timely than when it was first released. In this moment of crisis and awakening consciousness, the cultural zeitgeist is particularly ripe for *Conscious Evolution*. This new edition is a key "source text" for the emerging evolutionary worldview that is transforming our world.

— TERRY PATTEN, coauthor of *Integral Life Practice* and creator of the online series *Beyond Awakening: The Future of Spiritual Practice*

Foreword

B y now, few people can seriously doubt that we are moving through one of the most crucial and important periods in human history. The past twenty-five years have placed sufficient evidence before all of us. Political upheavals alone have overthrown (and that is an apt word) our longest-lived conventions and constructions. Add the social, economic, scientific, educational, and spiritual reorderings we are witnessing, and we have the recipe for much larger revolutions.

What makes this particular period so revolutionary is that people are now doing rather than simply watching all of this. They are taking hold of the apple cart and shaking the hell out of it. And that is exactly what they are trying to do: shake the hell right out of it.

This is a shakedown cruise. What we do and how we do it over the next few years will set the course for Spaceship Earth (as Buckminster Fuller so eloquently described it) for the next century and well beyond — if, indeed, the ship is allowed to survive at all. And it is her survival we are talking about here. I think most people now understand that.

I believe the human race is beginning to lose patience with itself, and with the way it has threatened its own existence. Those threats are still all around us, of course. But at least we now see them and realize that we have built them into our politics, our economics, our theologies, our social and educational systems. We are now ready to admit that our very way of doing things on this planet led us to this critical juncture, and so we are dismantling much of what we have put in place. This has produced some consternation among those who have become attached to the "old ways."

Not all of that concern is misplaced.

Our collective shift, our movement from observer to unwitting participant to conscious, cocreative cause in the re-creation of our combined experience, is what renders this time in our race's history so pregnant with possibilities — and dangers.

To what are we going to give birth? The paradise, at last, of which we have all so long dreamed, or the self-inflected damnations of our worst nightmares? Will we be successful in getting the hell out of our lives, or will we bring more of it in, until we finally destroy our planet altogether with one final foolishness?

Much will depend on how we respond to the challenges and invitations of this remarkable time, described and clarified in this sweeping book of breathtaking scope by Barbara Marx Hubbard. An urgent call from one of the most extraordinary visionaries of our time, *Conscious Evolution: Awakening the Power of Our Social Potential* is a document of stunning insight, including a blueprint for the re-creation of human reality so brilliantly and originally conceived, and so obviously and completely right, that it cannot help but propel the most ambitious among us to a new level of commitment to, and excited cocreation of, our future.

That is what is required now: Ambition. We must get off our collective duffs and arouse in ourselves a deep desire to produce our future, rather than wait to see what future is produced.

We have been asleep, and it is time for us to wake up.

Barbara Marx Hubbard — this incredible futurist, this breathtaking social seer — is the songbird of our new morning. This book is her melody. It is a tune to make the human heart sing, to make the soul dance again.

It is beautiful music to wake up to.

— NEALE DONALD WALSCH,
author of *Conversations with God*

Introduction

C *onscious Evolution: Awakening the Power of Our Social Potential* is an effort to respond to the immense challenges and opportunities of our age. It sets forth a vision of the vast transformational enterprise of the twenty-first century, and it seeks to discover the design of evolution inherent in all nature with which we can consciously cooperate to guide our actions. It is a design of how a planet makes its transition from its high-technology, polluting, overpopulating, and also ever-more-creative phase to a system that fulfills its collective potential. It reveals a spirit-motivated process of action based on the patterns of evolutionary success and suggests how we can ease the transition by identifying key ideas, processes, people, and activities now fulfilling elements of the emerging design of this new era of evolution.

Conscious Evolution carries us beyond the human potential movement into the social potential movement. It describes a holistic social architecture to enhance and connect social innovations that are now evolving our world toward social synergy, interconnectivity, and spirit-based compassion for all. *Conscious Evolution* identifies, out of the breakdowns in modern society, systemic breakthroughs demonstrating that we are in the midst of a positive quantum change — a metamorphosis of humanity consistent with the recurring patterns of 13.8 billion years of evolutionary transformation.

Conscious Evolution offers processes that can bring humanity across the dangerous threshold of possible self-destruction to gentle the shift already under way — to help us realize that we have the capacity to survive and grow far beyond our current condition. This vision for a wholesome transition process is composed of initiatives that are already occurring but have not yet been connected, communicated, and understood to be vital elements of a whole-system transition.

The pattern of action has five elements. Each element is vital to further "divining" the design of our transition.

The first element relates to the new story of creation. It is essential we understand that the universe has a history. Evolution's astonishing capacity for novelty, emergence, and transformation to ever higher orders of complexity, consciousness, and freedom has brought us from subatomic particles to our current condition, and it is still at work. It can be seen in the rise of new capacities and the commitment of millions of groups taking social action. It is felt internally as our heart's desire to be more, give more, love more, and create more — to evolve into a cocreative society where each person is free to be and do his or her best. Simply stated, the multi-billion-year trend of nature is to transform to more conscious life. We are the first few generations to become aware of evolution and of the fact that we are affecting our own future in our every act.

Through awareness of the recurring patterns in the process of evolution, we gain a new view of ourselves as active participants in the creation — cocreators within the process of evolution. The whole evolutionary journey is seen as the story of the birth of a universal humanity. Our current crises are understood as the crises of the birth of the next stage of our evolution, dangerous but natural. All of us on Earth are members of Generation One — the first to face crises and opportunities at this global scale, with no "elders" — no one who has made this evolutionary transition before — to guide us. We are facing radical newness, all together, whether we like it or not.

The second element requires us to understand and develop the new worldview called conscious evolution — evolution by choice, not chance. Conscious evolution is presented as a potent and ever-emerging idea of the nature of reality that can guide us in the ethical and creative use of our power toward the next stage of life.

The third element awakens our social potential. A new social architecture is presented whereby we can accelerate the connections among innovating people and projects to shift humanity toward a more positive future. How do we connect what works, in time to avoid the collapse of our social systems? Media and education to foster conscious evolution are presented.

The fourth element heralds the great awakening. A world-transforming series of events are described as a way to align our higher consciousness with our emerging capacities, to create a global mind and heart change and launch us through the twenty-first century with hope in our hearts. A vision of a cocreative society, what it may be like when everything works, is offered.

The fifth element invites you to participate by using the Evolutionary Spiral, the Wheel of Cocreation, and the SYNergistic CONvergence (SYNCON) process to cultivate social synergy. It also invites you to check out the online resources section of our Evolve.org website to guide your greater participation in helping to create an evolutionary community and to find partners and link with innovators in consciously evolving together.

Conscious Evolution is written specifically for those who have recognized the desire to transform and grow. It is a call to each generation to fulfill its creative potential. It provides tools and opportunities for each of us to participate in the greatest adventure in human history — our *conscious* evolution.

This is our finest hour. We live in a unique time, perhaps as significant as when the first humans arose in self-consciousness in an animal world. Millions of us are rising in a more universal, holistic, or cosmic consciousness in a still largely self-centered world. We are being called forth in every field and discipline to fulfill our potential through joining together in creative action. In the Gospel According to Thomas it is said, "If you bring forth what is within you, what you bring forth will save you. If you do not bring forth what is within you, what you do not bring forth will destroy you."

As we participate in this grand adventure, we will bring forth all that is within us and not only save ourselves, but evolve our world.

For me this book is an expression of my life — as a mother of five, grandmother of eight, futurist, lecturer, author, and spiritual and social explorer. In Thomas's words, it is a way of bringing forth what is in me, and I hope it will help to call forth what is within you.

My quest has been to understand and encourage our collective potential to evolve. All my adult life I have been exploring with colleagues throughout the world how we can have a graceful, peaceful, and gentle birth rather than the further violence and suffering that has been foreseen. *Conscious Evolution* is the fruit of this search.

I hope to continue serving as a catalyst for the social potential movement, in dialogue with people in every sector of society about how we can best apply the ideas of conscious evolution to our challenges and opportunities in health, education, environment, government, business, spiritual growth, and the arts and sciences. Equally important, I seek to embody the qualities of a cocreative human — at eighty-four as I write this revised edition — and to continue taking the sacred journey of a conscious evolutionary myself.

Within the next few decades we can and indeed must discover and commit to an evolutionary agenda and to a universal humanity where our spiritual, social, and scientific and technological capacities are fully activated. We are now in the midst of a global awakening that poses new dangers and new potentials. I believe that we will consciously and ethically learn to use our vast collective powers for the evolution of our species and the birth of a universal humanity. It is to this vision of our collective emergence that *Conscious Evolution* is dedicated.

PART I

The New Story
of Creation

CHAPTER ONE

The Awakening of Humanity

Occasionally in the course of human events, a new worldview emerges that transforms society. It happened when Jesus' disciples were inspired by his life to believe in radical transformation of the person and the world through love. It occurred in the Renaissance when the idea of progress through knowledge was born. It took place in the United States when the ideas of freedom and democracy became institutions through the Constitution and the Bill of Rights. It happened with the advent of the British Royal Society and the dawn of science through Copernicus, Galileo, and Newton, and again among the transcendentalists, such as Ralph Waldo Emerson and Walt Whitman, who believed that each individual is an expression of the divine, a free and sovereign person. Now, once again a new worldview is arising. This idea is the culmination of all human history. It holds the promise of fulfilling the great aspirations of the past and heralds the advent of the next phase of our evolution. It is the idea of *conscious evolution*.

Conscious evolution is occurring now because we are gaining

an understanding of the processes of nature: the gene, the atom, the brain, the origin of the universe, and the whole story of creation from the big bang to us. We are now changing our understanding of how nature evolves; we are moving from unconscious evolution through natural selection to conscious evolution by choice. With this increased knowledge and the power that it gives us, we can destroy the world or we can participate in a future of immeasurable dimensions. Into our hands has been given the power of codestruction or cocreation.

As Jonas Salk stated in *Anatomy of Reality*:

> The most meaningful activity in which a human being can be engaged is one that is directly related to human evolution. This is true because human beings now play an active and critical role not only in the process of their own evolution but in the survival and evolution of all living beings. Awareness of this places upon human beings a responsibility for their participation in and contribution to the process of evolution. If humankind would accept and acknowledge this responsibility and become creatively engaged in the process of metabiological evolution consciously, as well as unconsciously, a new reality would emerge, and a new age would be born.[1]

Consciousness has evolved for billions of years, from single cells to animals to humans, but *conscious* evolution is radically new. In *The Life Era*, Professor Eric Chaisson of the Wright Center for Scientific Education suggested that the second great event in the history of the universe is happening now.[2] The first event was when matter gained charge of radiative energy, which organized the explosive energy of supernovas into metals and materials that formed the material world more than 10 billion years ago. The second is when technologically competent human life gains an understanding of matter. As we learn how nature's invisible processes work, we can restore the environment of our Earth and free ourselves from poverty and disease; we can design new life-forms, bring life to other planets, and eventually explore and bring Earth life into the universe. Chaisson wrote in *ZYGON*: "The change from matter-dominance to life-dominance is the second of two preeminent events in the history of the universe....If our species is to survive and enjoy a future, then we must make synonymous the words future and ethical, thus terming our next grand evolutionary epoch, ethical evolution."[3]

Evolution or Extinction

An irreversible shift toward conscious evolution began in 1945 when the United States dropped atomic bombs on Hiroshima and Nagasaki. With this dreadful release of power we penetrated one of the invisible technologies of nature — the atom — and gained the power that we once attributed to the gods. This capability, combined with other rapidly developing technologies such as bio-technology, nanotechnology (the ability to build atom by atom), and artificial intelligence, if used in our current state of self-centered consciousness could lead to the destruction of the human race. We must learn "ethical evolution," as Chaisson said. And we do not have hundreds of years in which to learn.

The response to this crisis has been an uprising of a new consciousness — almost a new kind of humanity. Since the 1960s, the metamorphosis has accelerated as millions of people have become aware of environmental degradation, social injustice, and the need for radical change.

In *Blessed Unrest: How the Largest Movement in the World Came into Being and Why No One Saw It Coming*, Paul Hawken, a leading environmentalist and social change activist, examined the world-wide movement for social and environmental change. He discovered that groups working in these causes comprise the largest

movement on Earth, a movement that has no name, leaders, or
location and that has gone largely ignored by politicians and the
media. Like nature itself, it is organizing from the bottom up. Fun-
damentally, it is an expression of humanity's collective genius.[4]

As Hawken suggests, in the 1960s through the 1980s networks
of people in every field and sector of society formed to respond to
crises as well as to realize new opportunities. But we had no social
map of our collective potential. Although there were many positive social innovations, we didn't have a way to connect the dots.

We entered a period of confusion — a loss of vision and
direction. We continued to destroy our rain forests, pollute our
soil and water, and increase our rate of population growth. Our
global population is still rising. We cannot continue to increase
our population at the current rate and survive. If we continue
with our current practices, we may destroy ourselves. Many of us
have seen looming catastrophe, but few of us have realized that
this crisis is driving us toward positive change, toward a quantum
transformation.

Imaginal Cells

Let's compare our situation with the metamorphosis of a caterpillar into a butterfly. When the caterpillar weaves its cocoon, imaginal discs begin to appear. These discs embody the blueprint of
the butterfly yet to come. Although the discs are a natural part of
the caterpillar's evolution, its immune system recognizes them as
foreign and tries to destroy them. As the discs arrive faster and
begin to link up, the caterpillar's immune system breaks down
and its body begins to disintegrate. When the discs mature and
become imaginal cells, they form themselves into a new pattern,
thus transforming the disintegrating body of the caterpillar into
the butterfly. The breakdown of the caterpillar's old system is
essential for the breakthrough of the new butterfly. Yet, in reality

the caterpillar neither dies nor disintegrates, for from the beginning its hidden purpose was to transform and be reborn as the butterfly.

As Ferris Jabr wrote in *Scientific American*:

> Before hatching, when a caterpillar is still developing inside its egg, it grows an imaginal disc for each of the adult body parts it will need as a mature butterfly or moth — discs for its eyes, for its wings, its legs and so on. In some species, these imaginal discs remain dormant throughout the caterpillar's life.... Once a caterpillar has disintegrated all of its tissues except for the imaginal discs, those discs use the protein-rich soup all around them to fuel the rapid cell division required to form the wings, antennae, legs, eyes, genitals and all the other features of an adult butterfly or moth.[5]

By applying this analogy, we can see that during the 1960s our social systems started to become dysfunctional, or began to "disintegrate," as we experienced the Cold War and the threat to the environment, the growing population crisis, pollution, and social inequities. As people started waking up, they became imaginal discs in the body of society. The environmental movement, the antiwar movement, the Apollo space program, the women's movement, the civil rights and human rights movements, new music, Transcendental Meditation, yoga, and mind-expanding substances all encouraged a young generation to act as instruments of social transformation — striving to birth the still-invisible emerging world. But if we had been offered the opportunity to prematurely form a new kind of society, we would not have been ready. We were too young, too few, and too inexperienced to bring forth a more just, humane, and life-enhancing society at that time. And often when new leaders did step forward, they were attacked by society's immune system fighting to maintain the old social order of the caterpillar: witness the assassinations of Gandhi, John F. Kennedy, Robert Kennedy, John Lennon, and Martin Luther King, Jr.

The new social processes, structures, and systems to create environmental restoration, better education, universal health care, economic justice, alternative currencies, restorative justice, tolerance for social, sexual, and racial differences, and many other requirements of the coming age are just beginning to emerge. It may well be that our deep sense of life purpose, our callings, and our various passions to express ourselves are actually the still-dormant components of the emerging societal "butterfly," now in the process of metamorphosis. Our attraction to join with one another in specific groups and configurations may be the prepatterned requirement to find our appropriate partners with whom to cocreate our unique components of the whole-system shift now occurring.

Not only are millions of us developing ourselves as individuals in the spiritual and human potential movements, but we are just starting to organize new social functions in every major field, including health, education, environment, and governance. Yet we still are lacking a coherent social potential movement to connect what is already working and to guide us in the evolution of our communities and of society as a whole.

In the midst of this nascent uprising of wellness, innovation, and compassion, our basic social and economic systems have attempted to maintain the status quo despite the many warnings that the old ways, particularly in the developed world, were no longer sustainable. In many instances our existing systems are not humane; homelessness, hunger, disease, and poverty consume the lives of hundreds of millions of people and the environment continues to degrade. We can view the reactive and conservative ways of the past few decades as a survival mechanism — as the caterpillar's immune system rigidly holding on to old structures until new social systems are mature enough to function.

But the fact is that millions of people are now awakening in every field, culture, and ethnic group. The imaginal discs are linking up, are becoming imaginal cells, and are beginning to proliferate throughout the social body. Each person who says "I know I can be more," "I can do more," or "The world does not have to be this way" is an imaginal cell in the emerging culture of humanity. The social immune system is beginning to surrender as the new consciousness arises everywhere.

In *Global Consciousness Change: Indicators of an Emerging Paradigm*, Duane Elgin and Coleen LeDrew wrote:

> From this inquiry, we have concluded that a new global culture and consciousness have taken root and are beginning to grow in the world. This represents a shift in consciousness as distinct and momentous as that which occurred in the transition from the agricultural era to the industrial era roughly three hundred years ago.... This change in consciousness has two primary features. First, there is a further awakening of our unique capacity to be self-reflective — to stand back from the rush of life and, with greater detachment, observe the world and its workings non-judgmentally. Second, from this more spacious perspective, the Earth (and even the cosmos) are seen as interconnected, living systems.[6]

Cultural Creatives

It almost seems as though imaginal cells are beginning to gain ascendancy. This phenomenon is vividly presented in *The Integral Culture Survey: A Study of Transformational Values in America*.[7] Noted social analyst Paul H. Ray revealed through extensive research that there were 44 million "cultural creatives" in the United States alone in 1995 — almost one-fourth the American population. By 2008, that number had increased to 80 million adults, or roughly 35 percent of the American population.[8] Cultural creatives are defined by a set of values, a new lifestyle and worldview. Feeling that we are all members of one planet, they are concerned about the environment and social-economic justice. They have a different notion of relationship — one that is less hierarchical and more cocreative and participatory. They are interested in holistic health and are extending women's concerns into the public domain. Their emphasis is on transforming consciousness and behavior in all aspects of our lives — personal, social, and planetary.

Cultural creatives are social idealists, concerned not so much with political and economic power as those in the old movement were, but rather with seeking to change our image of the world, our sense of identity. Cultural creatives originated in the great social movements of the 1960s and are now maturing, taking their stand for a more spiritualized, personalized, and integrated culture worldwide.

According to Ray, cultural creatives are the fastest growing subculture in the United States, yet most of these creative individuals feel they are alone. They have not yet sensed their connection with one another or with the pattern and momentum of the collective change they represent. Nonetheless, as Marilyn Ferguson wrote in her seminal work *The Aquarian Conspiracy*, "A leaderless but powerful network is working to bring about radical change in the United States. Its members have broken with certain key elements of Western thought, and they may even have broken continuity with history."[9]

These are the imaginal cells of the social body. This emerging social potential movement is not revolutionary, but evolutionary.

Its aim is not to destroy, but to fulfill. When the butterfly emerges, it doesn't deny the caterpillar — it has actually consumed it! It is the caterpillar evolved. In this analogy, this movement is not an attack on another group or an assertion that "our way is better." Instead, we recognize that we have inherited enormous resources and intelligence from previous generations and that many of those resources can be repurposed now for the social good. The movement is not here to attack but rather to transcend and include the best of what has come before and to attract that which needs to come forth for the flourishing of our human and planetary potential. Its purpose is to evolve all of us, our communities, and our world so that all people are free to fulfill their highest potential.

Today, cultural creatives are communicating ever more rapidly with one another, affirming and reinforcing the new emerging pattern of more conscious living. Thousands of transformational workshops, trainings, and teachings are appearing in mainstream businesses, churches, and organizations. Books by new paradigm teachers and leaders consistently reach the bestseller lists. Through resonance, or echoing and reinforcing one another, values of inclusivity, spirituality, attunement with other species, ecological sensitivity, and social innovations are spreading. These values are not new; many are ancient, yet they are emerging now in a new way that is vital to the survival of the whole system.

This book is a call to those who are experiencing a deep motivation to be more, to find their life purpose and to contribute their gifts to the evolution of the world. Since the 1960s, countless such individuals have been maturing, yet mainstream media and our political system fail to adequately acknowledge them. These cultural creatives are rarely, if ever, at the heads of corporations, governments, or traditional religions because their current function is to evolve and expand systems, not to maintain or strengthen the current power structure as it is.

Although the desire for something more is widespread, often that something is not known. We lack a vision of what we want to create. Inquiries, conferences, and symposia throughout the world seek answers to major problems, yet something is still missing — we don't see where we are going; we have few positive visions of our next stage of evolution.

Our media, which are like a planetary nervous system, are far more sensitive to breakdowns than to breakthroughs. They filter out our creativity and successes, considering them less newsworthy than violence, war, and dissent. When we read newspapers and watch television news, we feel closer to a death in the social body than to an awakening. Yes, something is dying; however, the media do not recognize that something is also being born.

The Noosphere

A radically new phenomenon has emerged worldwide, and it is just now being more widely recognized. It is called the "noosphere" by Teilhard de Chardin in his famous work *The Phenomenon of Man*.[10] The root of the word is "noos," meaning "mind." The noosphere is the mind sphere, the thinking layer of Earth, the "global brain," the larger social body created by human intelligence. It is composed of all the spiritual, cultural, social, and technological capacities of humanity, seen as one interrelated superorganism. It is formed from our languages, our art and music, our religious and social structures, our constitutions, our communication systems, our microscopes, our telescopes, our cars, planes, rockets, laboratories, and more.

For Teilhard, the noosphere was actually the consciousness field of Earth. He believed that when infused with enough love and creativity, it would "get its collective eyes," and like the nervous system developing in a newborn baby, it would open its eyes.

Then we, as a newly born *planetary* culture, would see that we were one whole global body. As a Catholic, he called it the Christification of the Earth.

We as individuals have not changed much physiologically or intellectually in the past two thousand years, but our larger social body — the noosphere — has become radically empowered. We are now being born into an extended social and scientific capacity that has never before existed on Earth. It is through this collective social body of shared intelligence, capacities, and systems that we go to the moon, map our genes, clone a sheep, and transmit our words and images around the world at the speed of light. It is with this body that we codestroy or cocreate. It is into this body that our imaginal cells are born — the still-invisible, emergent societal butterfly. Conscious evolution has arisen at this precise moment of history because the noosphere has matured and has given humanity powers to affect evolution by choice.

We cannot see the noosphere. Neither our past philosophies or religions nor our social, economic, technological, or scientific systems have yet been able to encompass or guide the power of this collective body — a body that has been built by human endeavor and intelligence. With the advent of the idea of ethical and conscious evolution, however, we are beginning to discover a path of collaborative action that will lead us toward an immeasurable and positive future.

Without such a new and guiding worldview, further development of the planetary system will be increasingly distorted and destructive. If, however, we can see the glory of the noosphere maturing toward an immeasurable future for the human race — a future that attracts us, and calls forth our gifts — and if we can learn to collaborate even more effectively in bringing forward that future, we will then serve the purpose of awakening the whole body to its capacity.

The Social Potential Movement

The human potential movement began to come to public attention in the 1960s with the seminal work of Abraham H. Maslow, Viktor Frankl, Robert Assagioli, and others who discovered, nurtured, and affirmed the higher reaches of human nature. They developed techniques and practices to fulfill untapped human potential. In his seminal book, *Toward a Psychology of Being*, Maslow identified a hierarchy of human needs inherent in all of us. He said that we all have basic needs for survival, security, and self-esteem. When these basic needs are relatively well met, a new set of needs arises naturally. They are growth needs for self-expression in work that is intrinsically valuable and self-rewarding. Then, transcendent needs emerge: to be connected to the larger whole — one with Source — to transcend the limits of self-centered consciousness itself.[11]

Maslow had the genius to study "well" people rather than the sick and discovered that all fully functioning, joyful, productive, and self-actualizing people have one trait in common: chosen work or vocation that they find intrinsically self-rewarding and that is of service. If we do not find life purpose at the growth stage, he reasoned, we become sick, depressed, and even violent. People in modern society, he said, are stuck between survival needs and growth needs for further self-expression and self-actualization in a culture of intrinsic meaning.

Through the human potential movement millions of us have awakened, crossing the barrier from survival to growth needs. Yet, ultimately all of us want to find life purpose and meaning — a potentially huge community of people, perhaps a majority in the developed world (where basic needs are relatively well met).

The social potential movement builds on the human potential movement. It seeks to identify and map peaks of social creativity and works toward social wellness, a self-actualizing society, the same way the human potential movement cultivates the self-actualizing person. It seeks out social innovations and designs social systems that work toward a life-enhancing global society. I believe the social potential movement is on the threshold of a mass awakening, seeking to carry into society what individuals and small groups have learned spiritually and personally.

An Evolutionary Agenda

The social potential movement is the vital catalyst to carry us through the twenty-first century and to fulfill our collective potential in the third millennium. It is now surfacing in society and is ready for a shared vision that attracts and connects us, not only with one another but also with society as a whole. The time is ripe to move toward a new *evolutionary* agenda — not to reform but to transform based on the full and appropriate use of our immense new powers. This agenda is based on the hierarchy of social needs, which calls upon us to:

- meet basic food and shelter needs of all people;
- limit our population growth;
- restore and sustain Earth's environment;
- learn to coexist with other species;
- learn sustainable economic development and new forms of monetary democracy;
- shift the vast military-industrial-technological complex toward building new worlds on Earth and in space;
- redesign social and economic systems to enhance human compassion, cooperation, and creativity;
- emancipate individuals' unique potential and life purpose;
- explore and develop the further reaches of the human spirit and the universe beyond the planet of our birth;
- guide our radical new technologies, such as genetics,

nanotechnology, robotics, and space development toward evolutionary, life-oriented purposes.

What would happen if we began to use our new scientific and technological powers within such an evolutionary, open-ended agenda? Ancient prophecies have foreseen our self-destruction, but few of us have seen the magnificence of what we could become, collectively, through the use of all our powers — spiritual, social, scientific, and technological. In the past our glorious visions of the future — heaven, paradise, nirvana — were thought to happen after death. The newer thought is that we do not have to die to get there! We are not speaking here of life after death in some mythical heaven, but life more abundant in real time in history. We are discovering and participating in the next stage of our social evolution, the next turn on the Evolutionary Spiral.

A Spirit-Motivated Process of Action
for the Twenty-First Century

We now know that a pattern or design of action, also known as DNA, is encoded in the genes of every living organism and guides it from conception through gestation, birth, maturation, and death. From the study of epigenetics, we have also learned that the DNA code is a script that is influenced by the membrane or consciousness that surrounds the cell. It is not static and unchanging; it is responsive to its environment. Like the human body, planet Earth is a living system. Is it not possible, then, that there is a prepatterned (but not predetermined) tendency, an encoded design for planetary evolution, just as there is for biological evolution? And that our attitude, consciousness, and every action are affecting that life cycle?

As there is a biological cycle, it is also evident that there is a planetary life cycle. Earth's conception occurred with the big bang. The period of gestation included its 13.8 billion years of evolution, from its formation 4.5 billion years ago to the origin of human life. Its "birth," or collective awakening, is happening now as we begin to realize that we are one planetary body, capable of destroying ourselves or cocreating an immeasurable future, on this Earth and in the universe beyond. And we know that 4.5 billion years from now our sun will expand and destroy all the planets in the solar system. We live precisely midway in the life cycle of our planet. We have not yet seen another planet go through this change, so we have nothing with which to compare it. But let us imagine for the moment that we are a normal planetary event in the universe and that there is a pattern encoded in our collective spiritual, social, and scientific awareness, ready to be activated and affected by our actions, when the time for conscious evolution is here, just as the imaginal discs self-organize into new bodily functions when the caterpillar is ready to transform.

To awaken our magnificent social potential, we need first and foremost to become aware of our "new story," our evolutionary story. This story places us in the cosmos and reveals to us our vital part in the evolution of ourselves and our world.

I believe that the crises and opportunities we face today are triggering the next stage of planetary evolution and that we, as individual members of the planetary body, are now being awakened to our new personal and social capacities to participate in our evolution. This is not a plan imposed by any group or individual, but rather a design of evolution, a tendency toward a higher, more complex order and consciousness, with which we can cooperate and align ourselves to repattern our social systems and evolve ourselves.

CHAPTER TWO

Discovering the Importance
of the New Story

It was a cold November day in Paris in 1948 during my junior year abroad from Bryn Mawr College. Somehow I had separated myself from my classmates and wandered into Chez Rosalie, a small café on the Left Bank. A wood fire was burning and the smell of Gauloises cigarettes filled the air.

I sat at one of the wooden tables and ordered my lunch. A tall, handsome young American man opened the door, letting in the cold. There was only one place left for him to sit, opposite me. I smiled at him, immediately attracted, and introduced myself. He told me his name was Earl Hubbard. He had such a special intensity that I decided to ask him questions that had dominated my thoughts ever since the United States dropped the atomic bombs on Japan three years earlier, when I was fifteen years old, in 1945. My horror had stimulated these questions: What is the meaning of our new scientific and technological powers that is good? What is the purpose of Western civilization? What are positive images of the future commensurate with these new powers?

In my quest for answers, I had read through philosophy, science fiction, and world religions. But amazingly, except for brief glimpses in science fiction and mystical revelation, I found none. The philosophers looked back toward a golden age, as the Greeks did; or were cyclical, as in Eastern thought; or were stoical, believing there was "nothing new under the sun" as the Roman philosopher Marcus Aurelius said; or were existentialist, like Jean-Paul Sartre and Albert Camus, proclaiming that the universe has no inherent meaning except what we give it as individuals. Finally, I read the materialistic philosophers who proclaimed that the universe is nothing but matter and is inevitably degenerating to a "heat death" through increasing disorder or entropy as stars burn out, and with them all life will die. Although some visionaries and mystics foresaw a life beyond this life, beyond death, I found no positive visions of the future to work toward in *this* life.

With these questions I became a metaphysical seeker. My upbringing had been Jewish agnostic. I was a spiritual tabula rasa — a blank slate with no religious beliefs. When I asked my father "What religion are we?" he answered, "You are an American. Do your best!" But at what? I wondered. My father was a Horatio Alger type, a poor boy from Brooklyn who had become the toy king of the world. He told his children that the purpose of life was to win, to make money. But I couldn't believe him. I knew that even if everyone had money, everyone would be as frustrated as I was, seeking the meaning of life but finding nothing. Material comfort alone could not be the goal of existence. I had grown up with so many toys that by the age of six, I knew that more toys would not make me, or anyone else, happier.

If I did not know life's larger purpose, how could I know my own purpose? I felt an intense need for meaning and was obsessed with these questions, reading through world literature on a passionate quest to find an answer. I had asked my questions of every young man I dated. What is the purpose of our new powers? And what is your purpose? They had no idea! I never received a good answer — until that day in Paris.

We talked casually for a few moments, then I gained courage and asked the young man my question: What do *you* think is the meaning of our new power that is good? He looked at me with gray-green eyes, took a long drag on his Gauloises, and said, "I am an artist. My purpose is to seek a new image of humanity commensurate with our new power to shape the future."

I was stunned. There it was! A response to my deep life question. I was completely captivated by him.

I'm going to marry you! flashed through my mind... and I did.

As we sat at the little table that afternoon, the chestnuts roasting above a fire in the café, he explained that when a culture has a story everyone understands, it gives direction and meaning to that culture. When people no longer believe the story, the culture disintegrates.

For example, when the Homeric legends — the stories of the gods and goddesses, the heroes, the Trojan War — were written, fifth-century Greece was born. As time went on, the legends no longer seemed believable and a new story emerged. That story was the Gospels, which told of one man whose life and promise changed the world. We may never know the accurate history of Jesus' life, but we do know that the written story created a faith and expectation in the human heart that brought forth a new culture, one in which the individual is sacred, the kingdom of heaven is within us, and life everlasting is promised through love of God and one another. Christendom was born, and in a variety of forms it dominated the Western world for more than a thousand years. But gradually, with the advent of science and democracy some three hundred years ago, the literal interpretation of the Gospels was no longer possible for millions of people.

In the Renaissance a new story emerged. It was the story of progress through knowledge, through awareness of how nature works, and through the liberation of individual freedom. In 1486 Giovanni Pico della Mirandola wrote in *Oration on the Dignity of Man*, "We have made you a creature of neither heaven nor Earth, neither mortal nor immortal, in order that you may as the free and proud shaper of your own being, fashion yourself in any form you prefer."[1] Earl described the importance not only of a new story but also of a new image of humans. He vividly explained how the last great image of a human was in Michelangelo's famous sculpture *David*. He traced modern art through Manet, Monet, Pissarro, Picasso, and Jackson Pollock, ending in the art of the absurd, images of degradation and despair. We had lost not only our story but also our self-image.

From the Renaissance until the twentieth century the story of human freedom and progress had carried us forward. But as we sat there in the tragedy-laden environment of post–World War II Paris, we could see that the twentieth century so far had been the most violent and cruel in the history of humanity, with the destruction of millions of innocent people in wars and genocides perpetrated by the most sophisticated nations on Earth. The story of hope that had created the modern age seemed absurd. We knew that more of the same use of power and knowledge would destroy us.

In the postwar world, we were between stories — and we still are. We are wielding massive powers; we are overconsuming and overdefending while children starve and our environment and social systems deteriorate. Many say we have reached the point of "evolution or extinction." In the midst of our confusion, however, a new story of evolution is emerging that has the potential to inspire us to creative action.

Earl and I married. In our "breakfast dialogues," we began to

piece together this new story of our potential for conscious evolution. The story is coming from the combined insights of many
disciplines: scientific, historical, psychological, ecological, social,
spiritual, and futuristic. But it has not yet found its artistic or popular expression. We discover fragments in journals, poems, books,
lectures, conferences, seminars, and networks of those interested
in it. We see flashes in science fiction films. But it has not yet been
pieced together and told with the power required to awaken the
social potential within us and to guide us in the twenty-first century toward a future of infinite possibilities.

Understanding the new evolutionary story is a first critical
action necessary to carry us — without greater violence and suffering — toward a future equal to our full potential. Understanding gives us a sense of direction, hope, and meaning, providing us
with a new self-image and positive visions of a future we choose
and toward which our new powers can be used.

CHAPTER THREE

The Evolutionary Spiral

To understand our new story, we must look at our past as a movie of creation, a photogenesis, accelerated in time. It can best be visualized as an Evolutionary Spiral unfolding as one continuous process of transformation, from the origin of the physical universe — the big bang — through the formation of Earth, single-celled life, multicellular life, animal life, early human life, and now to us, going around the next turn of the Spiral, as described in *The Evolutionary Journey*.[1]

This story is not outside ourselves. It is within, as much as the process of our growth from a fertilized egg to a newborn infant is inherent in us. We are coded not only with the memory of our personal prenatal history, but also with our cosmic history. In *The Adventure of Self-Discovery*, psychologist Stanislav Grof asserted that consciousness "has the potential to reach all aspects of existence. This includes biological birth, embryonic and fetal development, the moment of conception, as well as ancestral, racial, karmic, and phylogenetic history."[2]

The experience of generations of existence lies in our genes. We are the product of 13.8 billion years of unbroken "success," the offspring of untold generations of procreative victories. We originated from the first cell and can cherish as our inheritance the efforts of ancestral organisms struggling through the sea and the air, over the land and the rocks, and in the trees — all of whom survived to reproduce.

We hold the mystery of this unbroken chain of life within our body-minds. Our blood and bones were formed from the material of Earth, which, in turn, was born of stardust. In our cells is the memory of the first life. In our brains are reptilian, mammalian, and early human experiences, as so beautifully described in Daniel C. Matt's *God and the Big Bang*.[3]

We are the universe in person. Our exquisite eyes originated in the first glimmer of light sensitivity in early cells. When we wake with fear in the middle of the night, our hair standing on the backs of our necks, our nervous systems are remembering the fear of unprotected animals. When we experience our own desire for transformation, we are feeling the universe evolving through us.

We can witness the new story of creation as the conception, gestation, and birth of a universal humanity capable of understanding the processes of creation and cocreating with them.

The New Story of Creation

UNIVERSE The new story begins in the Great Emptiness, the void, the field of all possibilities — the mind of God. Approximately 13.8 billion years ago, out of *no thing* at all, in one quantum instant appeared everything that potentially is. The spark of life that animates each of us was lit at the dawn of creation. In those first three seconds after the original "flaring forth," as cosmologist Brian Swimme called it in *The Universe Story*, the precise design was established that led to matter, life, self-reflective consciousness, and, now, our awakening to the whole process of creation.[4]

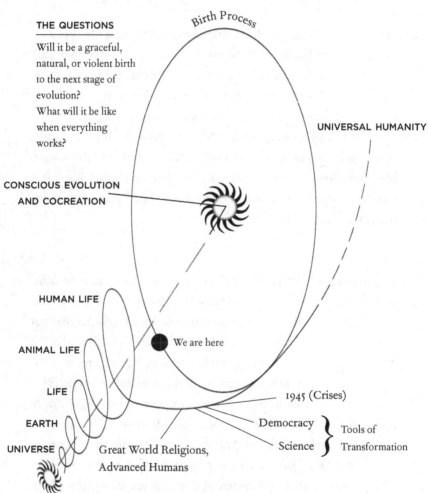

THE 13.8-BILLION-YEAR STORY OF OUR BIRTH

Birth Process

THE QUESTIONS

Will it be a graceful, natural, or violent birth to the next stage of evolution?
What will it be like when everything works?

UNIVERSAL HUMANITY

CONSCIOUS EVOLUTION AND COCREATION

HUMAN LIFE

We are here

ANIMAL LIFE

LIFE

1945 (Crises)

EARTH

Democracy

Science

} Tools of Transformation

UNIVERSE

Great World Religions, Advanced Humans

- Quantum transformation is nature's tradition.
- Problems are evolutionary drivers leading to innovation and transformation.
- Crises precede transformation.
- Holism is inherent in the nature of reality.
- Evolution raises consciousness and freedom through more complex order.

EARTH Our solar system and Earth were formed 4.5 billion years ago. Radiative energy condensed and became the metals and materials of our Earth.

LIFE Then, 3.5 billion years ago single-celled life appeared in Earth's seas. Sentient consciousness emerged. Life became semi-immortal — it divided to reproduce. For billions of years the seas filled with life, absorbing the nutrients of Earth.

At some point single-celled life hit a growth limit and began overpopulating, polluting, and stagnating. Faced with this threat, life might have attempted to adapt to limitations, but instead it innovated and transformed. The problem then became an evolutionary driver.

MULTICELLULAR Oxygen appeared, a poison to anaerobic cells.
LIFE In an extraordinarily complex process, a new form of organism evolved: multicellular life that could metabolize oxygen. With multicellular life a jump in consciousness occurred: animal consciousness emerged in the world of single cells. Evolutionary innovations of great significance appeared, such as sexual reproduction. Instead of dividing to reproduce, multicellular organisms learned to join their genes to create new life. The rudimentary beginnings of love were born. The joining of genes produced newness, diversity — the origin of the species. Yet, a more somber revolution occurred. Death entered the scene. Cells learned to degenerate and die. The offspring lived to reproduce anew. Diversity emerged. Sex and death are not eternal verities; they are evolutionary innovations

of tremendous value. They appeared in the process of evolution. And as we shall see, in our lifetime they are both evolving into a new form.

Hundreds of millions of years ago the first industrial revolution occurred, as space scientist Krafft Ehricke called it.[5] He claimed that the chlorophyll molecule was the first great evolutionary on Earth, and that the second was the human brain. Through the process of photosynthesis, the barren planet was colonized and the verdant biosphere emerged. Every nook and cranny filled with life. Out of the crises on early Earth, the next stage of evolution emerged.

HUMAN LIFE   Approximately 2.5 million years ago the earliest human species, *Homo habilis*, appeared — the next turn on the Spiral. Imagine awakening in the animal world with the first flickering of human awareness. Self-consciousness must have been unstable then, just as cosmic consciousness flickers on and off in us now. We must have sensed that we were different and felt separate and afraid. We became future oriented, foresaw our own death, and sought to overcome it. Death's ancient clock, set millions of years earlier at the dawn of multicellular life, was challenged by the human spirit, which sought to go beyond humanoid limits. We looked upward toward the stars and yearned for more, for a life beyond this life. We buried food with our dead. We had intimations of immortality. We listened for voices and heard signals from a legendary lineage of gods, from higher beings. The universe appeared alive.

Yet we were born into a natural system of both cooperation and fierce competition for survival. Millions of species are designed as biological weapons, consuming each other alive for

survival. For all our cruel behavior, however, humans were the
first to attempt not to kill, to try to preserve species, to bring compassion into the natural system. We inherited the natural trait of
carnivorous behavior, yet eventually felt guilty about killing.

Then an evolutionary flame of expectation ignited. The monumental struggle to overcome primitive conditions began. Through
tools, language, religion, art, and agriculture we strove for something new, something more. Goddess-worshipping cultures and
native peoples established a relatively peaceful, creative balance
with nature based on the equality of female and male, as described
by Riane Eisler in *The Chalice and the Blade*.[6]

Recently, about five thousand years ago, a glimmering of the next
turn on the Spiral arose with the great mystics who founded the religions of the world. They were future humans, foreshadowing what
is to come next through us. They began to attune to a higher reality, a spiritual impulse. The universal intelligence animating every
atom, molecule, and cell broke through into human consciousness.
Cosmic consciousness flickered in a self-conscious world.

Each culture on Earth is patterned at the core with the inspiration given by those advanced humans. Although there was a
violent shift away from more peaceful prehistoric societies, those
patriarchal religions set the ground for a quantum jump to the
next stage of human evolution.

In Egypt a whole civilization built pyramids to overcome
degeneration and death. They attempted to transform the pha-
raoh into a regenerating god, seeking eternal life.

In India the great yogis and teachers overcame the limitations
of self-consciousness and achieved cosmic, universal consciousness through yoga, or union with the All. They revealed that God
(Brahman) is the Supreme Spirit, the one infinite, eternal Presence — and that the manifestation of this Presence is the human
Spirit or Self.

In Greece the human mind penetrated the veil of matter and intuited the structure of the atom. The rudiments of science were born, the science now leading our generation to the discovery of our own birth narrative and of nature's invisible creative technologies — the atom, the gene, the brain — bringing us to the threshold of cocreation or codestruction.

In Israel the great evolutionary idea was grounded in Abraham's covenant with God for the promised land, a new heaven and Earth, a new Jerusalem. Humans were in partnership with God for the transformation of the person and the world, through obedience to the Law. Life seemed to have a direction. Among the Jewish people a new expectation of the transformation of the material world arose, setting in motion the drive toward the next turn on the Spiral.

Lao-tzu founded the Taoist religion in China, which is based on living in harmony with the great impersonal power (what we are calling the creative process of universal evolution). The sacred book of Taoism, the *Tao Te Ching*, teaches that heaven, Earth, and humans were created to be in harmony with one another, but that humans lost the way and created a world of disharmony.

Zoroaster, a Persian prophet, based his teaching on the one and only God, a supreme being of beauty, righteousness, and immortality.

Confucius believed in a supreme being, but placed the emphasis on our ethical relationships to one another to help us realize and understand the preordained harmony and justice of the universe.

Buddha achieved enlightenment and taught the Four Noble Truths: that reality is permeated with suffering; that attachment, or "thirst for permanence," is the cause of suffering; that the cessation of suffering is a possibility; and that there is a path that leads to the cessation of suffering.

Then, Jesus, born out of the vision and expectation of Israel, embodied the future human — beyond current *Homo sapiens* — with qualities now being awakened in us as we mature as imaginal cells. Jesus was an original cocreator, incarnating the creator, God. Jesus informed us that we, too, would do the work that he did and even greater work, in the fullness of time. He changed the image of God from one of power to one of love. He demonstrated what it means to be one with Source, incorruptible, with an unbroken connection to the process of creation, which he called Father, Abba, or intimate parent. His statement "I and my Father are one" (John 10:30), translated into evolutionary language, means "If you have seen me, you have seen the divine intelligence of the universe."

Jesus demonstrated the next stage of life with powers over the material world. He healed as easily as he breathed — effortlessly. He produced the loaves and the fishes in abundance. He calmed the weather. He revealed that through love of God and the other as oneself, he, and eventually we, could be radically transformed. He taught us that God is within all of us. We do not know what actually happened after the crucifixion, but the story tells us that he reappeared in a new body, resurrected, with continuity of consciousness — a body sensitive to thought, a light body that could appear and disappear, yet was tangible. In the story he transcended the human condition, representing a quantum jump in one lifetime.

Paul told us that the sufferings of the present cannot be compared with the glory that shall be revealed in us. "Behold, I show you a mystery, but we shall not all sleep, we shall all be changed" (1 Cor. 15:51). John wrote in the Revelation of the new Jerusalem, "and death shall be no more, neither shall there be mourning, nor crying, nor pain anymore, for the former things have passed away...Behold I make all things new" (Rev. 21:4,5).

These incredible messages of the next stage of human evolution spread like wildfire throughout the dying pagan world. Those who resonated with this possibility formed small groups and set in motion the expectation of a new life, in some future time, which I believe to be our current time. Expectation creates reality. As we believe, so it is done unto us.

Later Mohammed began teaching the belief in one God and the attainment of peace through submission to the will of God. The spiritual template for the next stage of our evolution was established. As Michael Grosso wrote in *Frontiers of the Soul*:

> The perspective I adopt features an evolutionary view of religion. Looking back in time, people may learn to see the earliest spiritual visions of the human race in a new light. They may come to see that the first products of the spiritual imagination were projected images of their own evolutionary future. From this perspective all the gods and goddesses, indeed, the whole pantheon of spiritual powers, become images of super-evolved humanity.[7]

From the perspective of the new story of creation, the great mystics who founded the world's religions are embodiments of different aspects of the future human. At least one visionary mystic or leader patterned each culture and cultivated specific qualities we now need to realize the next stage of our evolution: the mindfulness of Buddha, the Tao or Way of Lao-tzu, the yoga of the Hindus, the love of God and the Law of the Jewish people, the faith and obedience to Allah of the Muslim people, the understanding of community and Earth of native peoples and the Goddess tradition of prehistoric times, and Jesus' promise of radical personal and societal transformation through love of God and of the other as oneself. All these qualities, and many others, may be seen as evolutionary potentials in us, which are further activated as we approach the next turn on the Spiral.

More recently, two new tools of our transformation appeared: the scientific method and democratic institutions. Science is the mind's understanding of the processes of creation, such as the atom, the gene, and the brain. We penetrated the veil of nature, as the early Greeks did, but with a scientific method of investigation that began to reveal how nature actually works so that we could enter the process of creation ourselves. Out of science came technology, beginning the shift, as Eric Chaisson put it, from "matter-dominance to life-dominance" as we learned the laws of nature. We can release the power at the heart of the atom and build in miniature atom by atom as nature does through nanotechnology. We can alter our genetic code and create new lifeforms in laboratories. We seek to understand and reprogram the clock of death that was set with multicellular life hundreds of millions of years ago. We are extending our life spans, building new body parts, and even attempting to transfer our consciousnesses into computers to recreate ourselves in an advanced silicon-based life, which some believe will carry the human species in a new form into the galaxies.

The second great tool of our transformation is democracy. In the same time that the scientific method arose the ideas of freedom were set forth, especially in the United States in the Declaration of Independence, the Constitution, and the Bill of Rights. The New World called to pioneering souls throughout the globe to experience their freedom to worship, to build, to earn their living, to become fully themselves. The next phase of human potential was activated: the individual was set free from the categories of class and religion. Democracy provided the social architecture for the awakening of individual creativity en masse, which is necessary for the next stage of our emergence. Democracy set the stage for the awakening of the imaginal cells, and their freedom to self-assemble in specific "organs," or social disciplines, according to individual life purpose and attraction. This step marked the beginning of the social potential movement.

Through science and democracy we gained the power to affect nature and transform the world. But through our successes we began to overpopulate Earth and to pollute our environment. Corporations gained power to control the political system. When I graduated from Bryn Mawr College in 1951, one professor told me, "All our problems have been solved." We had no idea that there was a limit to growth or that there were pending environmental catastrophes. Many of us thought our purpose as women was to have as many babies as possible and to take care of our husbands and our homes. We were trying to preserve our lives and fulfill our dreams, following the two great human drives of self-preservation and self-reproduction. Few realized that we were heading for a global crisis of limits, that we would have to change our behavior or we would self-destruct.

We can have compassion for ourselves, for we did not know what the effect of our actions would be. Like those single cells in the seas of early Earth, we are running out of energy, resources, and space. We know that out of that crisis billions of years ago came mutation, evolutionary innovation, multicellular life, the biosphere, the origin of the species, and us!

If we had been a rock on Earth before life began and someone had said, "You, rock, are going to get up and walk and talk and fly to the moon!" could we have believed it? Yet here we are with new capacities bursting the very bonds of Earth. Can we imagine what may be emerging from our struggle? The answer is yes, for we can learn from the lessons of the past and apply them to our evolution now. One of the great values of knowing our story is to remember the amazing capacity of evolution to create new forms out of old.

We can see our Spiral as one continuous process of transformation. Although billions of species were extinct, nonetheless the direction of evolution continued. Each turning point on the

Spiral represents a breakthrough in consciousness and freedom. We can see the appearance of the great religions when sensitive humans were touched by the fire of Spirit at the core of the Spiral, coming in contact directly with the designing intelligence running through the whole process. We see the core of the Spiral as Spirit in action, the unmanifest manifesting in form, pressing each being to fulfill its potential and now breaking through in the minds of millions of humans, ready to more fully express Spirit in action in our own lives.

The Next Stage

The combination of science and democracy has led us toward the next stage of our evolution. The thinking layer of Earth, the noosphere, has matured. Let's visualize it now. Gregory Stock wrote in *Metaman*:

> The major evolutionary significance of humanity lies in the vast integrated entity it is creating rather than in the power of human beings as separated individuals.... Imagine looking down from the moon at the night side of an Earth pitch dark and invisible except for a brightly lit network of human constructions — luminous cities, highways, canals, telephone and power lines. A faint, speckled web of light would seem to float in space. Some regions of this lacework would form intricate geometric patterns, others would seem random and disconnected. Far from inert, this distant pattern of light would change and grow over decades, its shimmering fibers forming, extending, and joining in an almost vegetative fashion. This resemblance to life is not mere coincidence; the thin patina of humanity and its creation is truly a living entity. It is a "superorganism" — a community of organisms so fully

tied together that it is a single living being...although human centered, it is more than just humanity. [It] is also the crops, livestock, machines, buildings, communications, transmissions, and other non-human elements and structures that are part of the human enterprise.[8]

We are the humans who happened to be born as the noosphere connected and is on the verge of a collective awakening through us. In the past fifteen years, planet Earth has grown a new "nervous system" — Facebook, Twitter, the internet, and seven billion cell phones now connect us. We are like cells in the body of an infant who is being born. We are the ones who must consciously handle the fateful transition from one phase of our evolution to the next.

Let's sense ourselves now in this moment, feeling around us the crises of limits, the threat to our life-support systems, the pain of hunger, fear, and injustice, the expansion of capacities, the desire for self-expression, the search for a sense of direction and meaning — all the confusion of this modern time. The process is speeding up within us. Duane Elgin wrote in *Awakening Earth*:

> Because the pace of change is accelerating enormously, we should not assume that thousands or even millions of years will be required for us to achieve our initial maturity as a species. We have entered a time of explosive development... with each successive dimensional epoch there has been a dramatic collapse in the span of time required to move through a given stage....Evolution is quickening at a truly remarkable pace....In my judgment humanity has the potential to reach its initial maturity within another dozen generations, or roughly 500 years.[9]

Let's ask ourselves this key question: What is the significance of the next turn on the Spiral? What is happening to us now?

CHAPTER FOUR

Our Crisis Is a Birth

Let's rise up through the blue cocoon of Earth's atmosphere into the blackness of outer space and witness ourselves as one living system. Let's expand our sense of reality and see ourselves as members of one planetary body, struggling to coordinate ourselves as a whole. We see that we are gasping for breath as pollution chokes our lungs. We must handle our own wastes as toxins poison our air, our soil, our water, our bodies. We must shift to renewable, nonpolluting sources of energy. We feel the pangs of hunger increasing as population escalates and more and more of us are hungry. All around us our old life-support systems are breaking down. What worked before has become destructive. We do not have much time to change. We know that if we continue the behavior that worked so well in the past, we will destroy our chances for life.

This extraordinarily complex task has been thrust upon us for the first time in history, with "no operating manual for Spaceship

Earth," as Buckminster Fuller put it.[1] Yet, despite our fear and ignorance, we are learning to manage a planetary system.

Our crisis is a birth. We are one living system, and we have come to the limit of one phase of natural growth on a finite planet. We are growing beyond Earth's carrying capacities. We are told that we may have very few decades to survive, and that we are facing the sixth mass extinction in the history of the Earth, caused at least to some extent by our own actions. This is the greatest wake-up call that humanity has ever faced.

In *The Life Era*, Eric Chaisson suggested that perhaps the reason we have not yet met other high-technology species is because there are none.[2] These decades we are now undergoing — when a species hits its growth limits and gains the technological powers to destroy itself — are so dangerous that, he surmised, perhaps no other species has survived the transition. This idea is called the principle of cosmic selection, and, whether or not it is true, we must learn ethical evolution quickly.

We are in the midst of a massive upwelling of human potential, creativity, anger, and frustration. We are confused and reactionary, yet bursting with new capacities...just like a newborn child. Or, we may see ourselves as planetary midwives helping to deliver ourselves as a planetary system toward our next stage of life. As we seek to facilitate a gentle birth, a graceful and nonviolent transition to the next stage of our evolution, we will discover a natural pattern, a design of our birth transition, and develop a plan to cooperate with this design.

The Period of Our Birth

Let's examine the period of our birth and a few of its salient events. As we noted, the next phase of evolution began in 1945 with the explosion of the atomic bombs over Japan. We had gained powers we formerly attributed to gods. If we were to remain in self-centered consciousness and competition, we could destroy all life on Earth. This was a sign that the shift to the next stage of our evolution had begun: We would either evolve in consciousness or self-destruct our system.

Three key events stand out in the 1960s as critical to our birth transition. The first is the Apollo space program. Our species left the womb of Earth and set foot on the moon. We became physically universal in that we stepped beyond our biosphere and found on the moon and the asteroids the materials of a thousand Earths. Thus, solar energy and nonterrestrial materials could eventually provide resources for the physical growth of a universal species.

But the most immediate importance of the space program was not our potential for developing new resources and energy from space, or becoming a universal species ourselves. It was seeing the great picture of ourselves taken from the moon. Our first baby picture! Seeing ourselves as one magnificent globe of life floating in the blackness of space triggered the second great event during the period of our birth: the awakening of the environmental movement. In 1970, only one year after the lunar landing, the first Earth Day occurred. Suddenly, millions of us fell in love with our Earth as a whole. We saw that the environment is not something separate from ourselves. It is our extended body. We are all connected. What the mystics had told us from time immemorial became a pragmatic fact. We are all members of this planetary body. We fell in love with ourselves as a whole. It was impossible to love our North and not our South, our East and not our West. A spontaneous joy coursed through the planet. People became passionately concerned about the trees, the air, the animals, the water, the ozone layer, and more. A growing number began to take responsibility for nature as a whole and for other species because they were part of ourselves. Our birth process matured as we struggled to preserve and evolve our life-support systems as well as coexist consciously and compassionately with other species.

A third crucial event of the 1960s was the awakening of women en masse to a new identity, a new function, a new role in evolution. Suddenly, in one generation we saw that our age-old function of massive reproduction had to stop. We began shifting from the all-consuming and heroic effort of birthing and nurturing five or ten children to the newer effort of finding self-expression and meaningful work — moving from the first two basic human drives for self-preservation and reproduction toward self-evolution and cocreation.

We seek now to fulfill our vast and yet untapped potential as individuals and as a species capable of conscious evolution. We are shifting from procreation toward cocreation and chosen children, from the effort of giving birth to many children to the equally demanding work of giving birth to our full potential selves and our work in the world. Feminine energy is being liberated by the population crisis to express itself for the sake of the larger human family and all life on Earth — and just in time. For in feminine creativity lie innovations, gifts, and vital contributions to our social potential movement and to the evolution of humanity.

In one extraordinary decade we learned that we are physically universal, and we recognized that we are all members of one planetary body and must care for ourselves as a whole. In addition, one-half the human race began to change its function from maximum procreation to something new! We went from self-reproduction toward self-evolution. These events, along with many other significant breakthroughs, marked the period of our birth, comparable perhaps to the first few days after a biological organism is born.

Meanwhile, our planetary nervous system, our media, have begun to link us up as one interfeeling, interacting body. Although we may not always be aware of it, during this extended period there has been a continuous and massive effort to connect through our hearts. In 1985 "Live Aid," the television broadcast on the theme of hunger, connected us for eighteen hours and was viewed by nearly two billion people. Compassion for the suffering of others awoke in our hearts as popular musicians sang Michael Jackson and Lionel Richie's "We are the world, we are the children."

John Randolph Price, in his book *The Planetary Commission*, asked for a "healing of this planet and to the reign of spiritual love and light in this world — with no less than 50 million (one percent of the human race) — meditating at the same time on December 31, 1986."[3] And the first World Healing Meditation occurred at noon Greenwich mean time.

If the universe is really more like a thought than a thing, as physicist John Wheeler has said, and if we are indeed the "universe in person," then we may say that the universe itself began to think the thought of peace and harmony on Earth. In 1987 the Harmonic Convergence sent millions to resonate with sacred places on Earth. At dawn people went to mountains, to groves, to parks, to pyramids, and to temples to empathize with the living Earth. Empathy for one another and for nature charged the global mind with love. During the event I was in Boulder, Colorado, with Jose Arguelles, the originator of the Harmonic Convergence. He said to me, "Barbara, the world will never be the same again."

In 1988 Gorbachev went to the United Nations and called for cooperation and even cocreation. No one can claim a direct cause and effect between mass events of love and peace and global change, but nonetheless it is true that the world was never the same again.

In the 1990s the Communist empire crumbled, falling of its own weight as people struggled to find their own way in freedom. The Berlin Wall came down. Television communicated the joy, the liberty, the hope to billions of us simultaneously. Celebration spread throughout the social body. Not predicted by leaders and experts, a nonviolent, people-motivated revolution had occurred. (Those who had been citizen diplomats in the Soviet Union meeting with its brilliant, creative people seeking freedom were not so surprised.)

Millions were liberated from the largest totalitarian dictatorship the world had seen. Communism was defunct, overcome, yet liberal democracy and capitalism were foreign systems, especially in Russia, and were also showing their limitations in the West. New social forms that might actually lead toward a more holistic, cooperative, freer world had not yet emerged. There was as yet no well-established third way between communism and capitalism. The social potential movement was still too young. Yet, movements for peace grew. Apartheid fell in South Africa. New groups became empowered. The idea of equality of races and sexes, of ignored or suppressed minority groups, gained respect. The very idea of war was seen as immoral, even though we still armed ourselves and fought.

But as the world became more integrated and dictators lost their grip, previously suppressed groups sought greater individualization. Each group, nation, culture, sexual preference, race, creed, and color wanted to assert its identity. The rise of nationalism, ethnicism, and political correctness surprised a world that many felt was ready to become a global village. We sought identity in our ethnic or racial roots and overlooked our common roots in the cosmos and our common destiny as a universal humanity. We did not see that we were on the threshold of a planetary birth, a next stage of human evolution. Instead, we became regressive and turned against ourselves, rather than looking forward together. Something vital was missing. There was — and still is — no common story or vision of the future to attract us.

Meanwhile, the United States had lost its enemy. The vast

military-industrial-technological complex no longer has a common threat. It sits poised, with no mission equal to its immense evolutionary capacities, with thermonuclear bombs and other technologies that can destroy the world many times over. Disaffected groups rise up to threaten powerful nations and peoples. Global corporations of inordinate power span the Earth and mine its resources while the environment degrades and millions starve. The electronic media connect us, and the internet allows us to communicate individually and collectively. Yet we have no shared consciousness. It is a moment of transformation toward devolution or evolution.

The Collective Rise of Consciousness

Let's imagine that we are planetary diagnosticians, called in to assist in this period of our birth. What do we see? We find ourselves to be a brilliant species with artistic, spiritual, scientific, and technological genius. We are the jewel of our solar system, budding with genius and creativity, ready to grow. The vast majority of our members are good; we care for our young and strive to follow an ethic of consideration for others. Yet the history of our species is brutal, tragic in the cruelty we have afflicted upon one another, upon other species, and upon Earth herself. This flaw, this sense of separation from one another, from nature, and from Spirit, is the essence of evil behavior.

Our situation has come to a critical stage. Are there some heretofore hidden processes in us that we could activate, some homeopathic remedies for our violence that could stimulate more empathy, connectedness, and love?

Peter Russell estimated in *The Global Brain Awakens* that "10 billion seems to be the approximate number of units required in a system before a new level of evolution can emerge."[4] Coincidentally, it takes approximately 10 billion atoms to make a cell and 10 billion cells to make a brain. A UN report entitled "World Population Prospects: The 2012 Revision" estimates that we will reach nearly 9.6 billion by 2050.[5]

Is 10 billion people what it will take for us to feel that we are all connected? But this is already a fact. We *are all* connected. Does it actually take a certain density of neurons on the planet for us to *feel* it and to overcome the illusion that we are separate from one another, from nature, and from the great creating process that is now flowing through us?

Here is a fascinating comparison with what happens to a newborn baby just after birth and what may happen to a planetary organism just after its birth period. At first the baby does not know that it has been born. Then, at some unexpected moment, after it has struggled to coordinate itself and nurse, stimulated by this effort its little nervous system links up and, suddenly, it opens its eyes and smiles at its mother. In that radiant smile it signals that it knows, at some deep level, that all is well, that it can survive and grow.

Here we are, from the perspective of the new creation story, a planetary species just after birth, struggling to coordinate ourselves as a whole, fearing the destruction of our life-support systems, confused, and afraid. Nonetheless, our planetary nervous system is linking us up through phones, faxes, global satellites, and the internet. Are we being prepared for a time in the not too distant future when we will have an actual, empathic experience of our oneness? Are we possibly at the threshold, as a newly emerging planetary organism, of our first *planetary smile*, a mass linkup of consciousness now emerging in so many: an awareness that we are whole, we are one, we are good, we are universal? Is this sense of connectedness and wholeness a vital part of the design we can facilitate? I believe the answer is yes and that it can become the catalyst and be fostered by us, as shown later in this book.

Rupert Sheldrake, the British plant biologist, proposed in *A New Science of Life* that systems are regulated not only by the laws known to physical sciences, but also by invisible morphogenetic fields.[6] His theory suggests that if one member of a species performs a certain behavior, it affects all others ever so slightly. In a famous experiment rats trained to run a maze in one laboratory seemed to affect the learning rate of rats in a completely separate laboratory who learned to go through the maze more quickly after the first group did so. If a behavior is repeated long enough, its morphic resonance builds up and begins to affect the entire species. What began with the great mystics may be accelerating in us because of the crises and opportunities of our birth, thereby awakening the imaginal cells to their new functions, their organic partners, their untapped potentials. We may have entered what Peter Russell called a phase of "super-exponential growth, leading to a chain reaction, in which everyone suddenly starts making the transition to a higher level of consciousness." He wrote in *The White Hole in Time*:

> Could it be that in much the same way as the destiny of matter in a sufficiently massive star is to become a black hole in space, the destiny of a self-conscious species — should it be sufficiently full of love — is a "spiritual supernova"? Is this what we are accelerating toward? A moment when the light of inner awakening radiates throughout the whole? A white hole in time?[7]

Five Lessons of Evolution

To help answer Russell's questions and to discover the greater design of evolution, let's look backward to see if we can learn from the patterns of past quantum jumps to help us through the traumatic period of our birth and the next turn on the Evolutionary

Spiral. By reviewing our new story, we gain five major lessons that will encourage us to move forward now. The historical perspective of a few thousand or even million years is not enough time to see the recurring patterns in cosmic evolution. When we stand back and witness the unfolding story — the big bang, energy, matter, galaxies, planets, Earth, life, animal life, early human life, and now another transformation — the logic of our hope is revealed, guidelines are given, and patterns of our transformation become visible.

1. Quantum transformations are nature's tradition. "Quantum" in this context means a jump from one state to the next that cannot be achieved through incremental change alone. The jump from nonlife to life or from the most intelligent animal to early human is an example of quantum transformation. Infinitesimally small differences eventually lead to discontinuity and newness. The capacity of evolution to produce radical newness is truly astonishing. One hundred thousand years ago there were no *Homo sapiens*; a few million ago there were no early humans. Before that there was no biosphere and no Earth, and 13.8 billion years ago there was no material universe. Nature works through radical change.

2. Crises precede transformation. When nature reaches a limitation, it does not necessarily adapt and stabilize; it innovates and transforms, as we saw with the single-cell crisis. Problems are often evolutionary drivers vital to our transformation. We learn to look for innovations that the problems are stimulating. We view our problems positively and notice the transformations occurring around us. For example, the threat of nuclear weapons is forcing the human race to go beyond all-out war. The environmental crisis is awakening us to the fact that we are

all connected and must learn how to manage a planetary ecology or else destroy our life-support system. We learn to expect the unexpected and to anticipate the new.

3. Holism is inherent in reality. Nature takes jumps by forming whole systems greater than and different from the separate parts. Subatomic particles form atoms, atoms form molecules, molecules form cells, cells form multicellular animals, on and on to humans — one of the most complex organisms on Earth, as Jan Smuts pointed out in his seminal work, *Holism and Evolution.*[8] We see that planet Earth is herself a whole system. We are being integrated into one interactive, interfeeling body by the same force of evolution that drew atom to atom and cell to cell. Every tendency in us toward greater wholeness, unity, and connectedness is reinforced by nature's tendency toward holism. Integration is inherent in the process of evolution. Unity does not mean homogeneity, however. Union differentiates. Unity increases diversity: We are becoming ever more connected as a planet while we seek further individuality for our cultures, our ethnic groups, and our selves.

4. Evolution creates beauty, and only the beautiful endures. Early species are often ungainly, like the *Eohippus* or *Homo erectus* as compared with a magnificent horse or a beautiful human. Every leaf, every animal, every body that endures is exquisite. Even creatures we may consider dangerous or disgusting are beautifully made. The process of natural selection favors elegant, aesthetic design. (This gives us courage as we recognize the crude forms of so many modern cities, houses, and machines.) If this tendency of nature continues through us, the creations of

human nature will become ever more ephemeral, minia-
turized, and beautiful.

5. Evolution raises consciousness and freedom. This lesson
   is the most important of all. Teilhard de Chardin called
   it "the law of complexity/consciousness."[9] As a system
   becomes more complex — from nonlife to life, from
   single cell to animal, from animal to human — it jumps
   in consciousness and freedom. Each is a jump through
   greater complexity and interconnectivity. Our planetary
   system is becoming more complex. We are being connected by our media, our environment, our powers of
   destruction. If we were to drop a nuclear weapon on an
   "enemy," the fallout would kill us. If a child starves in
   Africa or a youth is shot in Los Angeles, we immediately
   feel it in our homes through television and the internet.
   This globalization is awakening in us a whole-system
   consciousness to complement the more mystical, unitive,
   or cosmic consciousness. This consciousness, a synthesis
   of both inner and outer connectedness, is still unstable in
   us, as perhaps self-consciousness and individual awareness were unstable in the animal world. Yet, the tendency
   toward expanded consciousness and freedom is the direction of evolution itself.

The five lessons of evolution provide a response to the crisis
of meaning we face in this postmodern world. As business visionary Mark Donohue said to me in a personal conversation in 1998:

Today we are beginning to discover a systems perspective to guide our new capacities, one that respects the
13.8-billion-year history of successful transformation.
Many of us realize that there is an implicate pattern of
success, that we are not random events cast on the seas of
time, that we are now cocreative with evolution itself. We

no longer need to solely be reactive to our problems. We can be proactive and choose a future commensurate with our self-evident capacities.

These lessons do not mean we will inevitably succeed. Evolution is a contingency, not an inevitability. We become potentialists, not optimists. We see the potential for evolution in the system, and in understanding our possibilities we take appropriate action. From this time forward, evolution proceeds more by choice than by chance.

Universal Humanity

UNIVERSAL
HUMANITY

Currently, there is a wide range of opinion as to whether we are declining rapidly and perhaps irreversibly toward irreparable global environmental or economic catastrophe, or whether our crises are leading us toward a positive future. Both scenarios, as well as many variations, are possible. The purpose of this book is to discover a plausible positive scenario that attracts us to work toward it. For as we see reality, so we act, and as we act, so we tend to become.

The next turn on the Evolutionary Spiral is a quantum jump, yet there are signs that we are moving toward a positive future in the short range, which could make the transition from this stage of evolution to the next far less traumatic.

Let's imagine that such a positive trend is unfolding. The noosphere is maturing; we are appreciating our new evolutionary story; cultural creatives and conscious evolutionaries are proliferating and connecting; new technologies show promise of providing nonpolluting, renewable energy; and new social systems are emerging that reinforce cooperation and creativity. Imagine that coming forth out of these advances is a quantum jump toward the next stage of our evolution.

In *Creating Your Future*, David Ellis recommended that we choose a long-range future, five hundred to one thousand years ahead, beyond even the lifetimes of our children's children.[10] In this exercise we free ourselves from self-imposed limits and allow our deeper evolutionary intuition and desire to rise to consciousness. This expression then forms a magnetic field to pull us forward toward what we choose. This future is ourselves revealed, our potential manifested. Our future pulses in us as the oak tree animates the acorn.

As we seek this vision, we have the lessons of evolution to guide us, and they show us that our evolution is the expression of a 13.8-billion-year trend toward higher consciousness, toward greater freedom through more complex order, despite five mass extinctions and species failures. We have the passionate desire within our hearts to be our full potential selves. If we can make it through this period of our birth, if enough of us can learn ethical evolution, the future for humanity would be unlimited. We can imagine that in the next thousand years humanity will be acting out the promise, first laid down in the early religions, for paradise, for a new heaven and a new Earth in our evolving world.

Here, we just catch glimpses of our potential to allure us, to charm us and beckon us forward to experience it. In the seeing comes the believing, comes the acting upon what we see. Our image of the future is instrumental in the evolution of the world. This is what *conscious* evolution means.

Let's join together in choosing the best and most glorious future possible. Let's imagine the good we can do by working harmoniously. Each of us will see it differently, and each has a vital contribution to give. Later in the book we will flesh out these visions. Now, let's just catch a glimpse of ourselves as a universal humanity with our spiritual, social, and scientific capacities working toward higher consciousness and greater freedom through more complex order.

Coming Attractions

We can imagine that cosmic consciousness has been secured. Those peak moments of higher awareness we have felt in flashes throughout human history are now stabilized, as self-consciousness was stabilized in the animal world when humans first appeared. The new morphogenetic field of higher consciousness eases our transition from self-centered to spirit-centered humanity. We are connected to Source, not as creatures but as cocreators. The universal intelligence that flows through every particle in the universe is now conscious in us.

Through a combination of medical advances and the healing arts we are fully in touch with our body-minds and are becoming self-healing and self-regenerating. The extraordinary powers of mystics and healers become a normal capacity in all of us.

Our extended electronic nervous system has linked us up as one inter-feeling, interacting global organism. The global brain has turned on, and each of us has access to the knowledge of the whole system. Our intelligence has taken a quantum turn.

Our infant space programs have matured. As once the process of photosynthesis created the biosphere, now humans are creating the "humansphere" in outer space. As we reach our growth limits on Earth, we preserve and conserve life here while learning to extend life beyond our home planet. NASA engineer Kenneth Cox suggested a Third Millennium intention: "To create a permanent living presence throughout the solar system and seek value and meaning for humankind in Earth/Space. To establish human settlements in Earth orbit, on planetary surfaces, and in other appropriate orbital space. To live, work, and prosper in multiple space communities in the solar system, and develop a virtual presence beyond our 'local Earth-Moon-Sun universe.' "[11]

The stabilization of unitive consciousness combined with the extension of human habitats in space, increased intelligence through our maturing global brain with enhanced health and life extension supported by new technologies for nonpolluting energy such as solar-, hydrogen-, and vacuum-based energy, synergistic, win-win social systems and other innovations will radically alter the human condition. These capacities will be the conditions in which the social potential movement comes to fruition. Each person born into this extended spiritual, social, and physical environment will be a member of universal humanity. Our vast, untapped human potential will be called forth in an enriched noosphere as we engage in utterly new vocations and functions in the evolving social body. All of us will be free to be and do our best.

What is in store for us, if we can make it through this crisis of our birth, will make our hearts leap with joy now. It is a vision of the birth of a universal species, a quantum jump from *Homo sapiens* to *Homo "universalis,"* from the self-conscious human to the cosmic conscious, cocreative human.

Is it possible? Yes.

Can we do it? It depends on what you and I do now, in the next few decades, in this most critical period following our birth. We are on the threshold of *conscious* evolution — the next vital element in the life design.

PART II

Conscious Evolution
A New Worldview

CHAPTER FIVE

Conscious Evolution

Deep in the hidden process of our metamorphosis we can see a natural design — an evolutionary pattern to guide us toward the next stage of transformation. We intuit the presence of the still-invisible societal butterfly, yet how do we become it? What we are seeking is a worldview that will call forth our creative action and direct our immense powers toward life-oriented and evolutionary purposes. That guiding worldview is, I believe, conscious evolution. It holds that through our unprecedented scientific, technological, social, and spiritual capacities we can evolve consciously and cocreatively with nature and the deeper patterns of creation (traditionally called God), thus enabling us to manifest a future commensurate with our unlimited species and planetary potential.

Conscious evolution as a worldview began to emerge in the latter half of the twentieth century because of scientific, social, and technological abilities that have given us the power to affect the evolution of life on Earth. Conscious evolution is a metadiscipline;

the purpose of this metadiscipline is to learn how to be responsible for the ethical guidance of our evolution. It is a quest to understand the processes of developmental change, to identify inherent values for the purpose of learning how to cooperate with these processes toward chosen and positive futures, both near term and long range.

This worldview is the fruit of all human history and the opening of the next stage of human development. It has come into focus midway in the life cycle of our planet with the maturation of the noosphere. Conscious evolution is awakening in humans. Like imaginal cells nearing the time of metamorphosis, we are just beginning to self-assemble into various new social organs. We are guided intuitively by a vision of a new life to come and a desire to fulfill unique creativity in the cocreation of that new life.

The Second Great Event

As mentioned earlier, conscious evolution heralds the second great event in the history of the universe. We are not speaking of some minor new idea but of an advance in the evolution of evolution itself. Eric Chaisson wrote in *ZYGON*:

> Technologically competent life differs fundamentally from lower forms of life. We are different because we have learned to tinker not only with matter but also with evolution. Whereas previously the gene and the environment (be it stellar, planetary, geological, or cultural) governed evolution, we humans on planet Earth are rather suddenly gaining control of both these agents of change.... We now stand at the verge of manipulating life itself, potentially altering the genetic makeup of human beings [and even cloning ourselves]. We are, in fact, forcing a change in the way things change.... The

emergence of technologically intelligent life on Earth, and perhaps elsewhere, heralds a whole new era, a Life Era. Why? Because technology, for all its pitfalls, enables life to begin to control matter, much as matter evolved to control radiative energy more than 10 billion years ago.

Though a mature Life Era may never come to pass, one thing seems certain: Our generation on planet Earth, as well as any other neophyte technological life forms populating the universe, is now participating in an astronomically significant transformation. We perceive the dawn of a whole new reign of cosmic development, an era of opportunity for life forms to begin truly to fathom their role in the cosmos, to unlock the secrets of the Universe, indeed to decipher who we really are and whence we came.... The implications of our newly gained power over matter are nothing short of cosmic....As sentient beings we are currently beginning to exert a weighty influence in the establishment of a "universal life" with all its attendant features, not least of which potentially include species immortality and cosmic consciousness.[1]

The capacity for conscious evolution means that our species has become capable of understanding, resonating with, and consciously incarnating the processes of creation itself. Already we can fathom the miracle of cosmogenesis — the story of the evolution of the cosmos. We can reach into the heart of nature and see the invisible workings of creation — the atom, gene, brain, ecological systems, stars, and galaxies. Spiritually we are attuning to the patterns of evolution within us as we begin to transcend the illusion of separation born out of the phase of *self*-conscious humanity. As we do so, we internalize and embody the impulse of evolution, the tendency in evolution toward greater complexity, consciousness, and freedom.

Whether or not there is other life in the universe, our role, if we learn conscious evolution, is to become partners in the process of creation, enhancing life on Earth and bringing Earth's life into the universe. We rightly stand in awe of the magnificence of cosmogenesis as well as in reverence for ourselves as creatures of this monumental process.

As Catholic scholar Beatrice Bruteau wrote in "Symbiotic Cosmos," in a chapter entitled "Holy Technology":

> From having felt completely at the mercy of the natural world, we begin gradually to feel in a position of power over the natural world. There is a third stage of this development, and that is the sense of the natural world itself producing beings that can so intelligently and freely and creatively manipulate the natural world. We ourselves are products of the self-making world, and what we do by our technologies is continue the self-making of this world. When the technologically changed environment has in turn changed us, then we must see that this also is part of the self-making of the world.
>
> Human extensions by means of technology are not to be opposed to "Nature." They are themselves part of what Nature is doing. It is the Cosmos itself, as the human being, that is doing these things as its own autopoietic (self-creating) development...and there is nothing riskier than creating a world so that it can grow up to be free and creative itself — I think that we must see our technology as something holy, as part of — at the moment, the vital advancing edge of the autopoietic, symbiotic cosmos.[2]

There is no hubris in the concept of conscious evolution — no pride that humans alone, by willful decision for selfish ends, with no regard for the laws of nature or the relationship with other species, can guide the process of change. We can clearly see that such self-centered behavior will destroy us. Conscious evolution inspires in us a mysterious and humble awareness that we have been created by this awesome process of evolution and are now being transformed by it to take a more mature role as cocreators. In this view we do not stand apart from nature, but, rather, we are nature evolving.

Nor is the concept anthropocentric. From the perspective of conscious evolution, *Homo sapiens*, in our current phase, is a transitional species. We are not viable in this state of separated consciousness with so much power. We will either evolve or become extinct.

Yet, we are advancing toward conscious evolution with every new discovery made by the collective efforts of hundreds of thousands of individuals. In the biological revolution, in the healing arts, in humanistic, transpersonal, and spiritual psychologies of growth, in social innovations in the fields of health, education, and the media, in business, science, and the arts, we are learning new abilities to cocreate with nature. And we are doing so based on human nature's intentional motivation, not as passive experiencers but as conscious participants of and codesigners with evolution. In fact, we *are* evolution becoming self-aware.

The History of Quantum Change

How do we know that conscious evolution is the next quantum jump? We don't. Yet we do know, from the history of quantum transformations, that such radical change will eventually occur. Our evolutionary history has a long heritage of astonishing innovations. Let us remember, it is the nature of nature to transform, especially when life hits a growth limit.

I believe that the capacity for conscious evolution is a design innovation comparable in importance to other major evolutionary innovations. Let's briefly review the extraordinary history of quantum changes through design innovations, to gain a deeper insight into the potential of our capacity.

The design innovation that formed matter and Earth was the synthesis of the elements — from hydrogen and helium to iron and gold. It took billions of years for nature to create a way to synthesize radiative energy to form the metals and minerals that make up our bodies today. Out of formless, shimmering gasses and explosions of supernovas the elements were formed, condensing light and motion into matter and providing the substance of all subsequent evolution.

For the origin of human life, the design innovation was the genetic code — DNA intelligence — the exquisitely complex information at the heart of every cell coded with instructions that build our bodies. This nearly invisible information system coiled in the strands of our DNA holds the memory of the entire evolution of life and, some believe, the coding for further life to come. Timothy Leary stated this controversial hypothesis in *Info-Psychology: A Manual on the Use of the Human Nervous System According to the Instructions of the Manufacturers*:

> The DNA code contains the blueprint of the past and the future. The caterpillar DNA contains the design for construction and operation of the butterfly body. Geneticists are just now discovering "unused" sections of the DNA, masked by histones and activated by non-histone proteins, which are thought to contain the blueprint of the future. Evolution is not a blind, accidental, improvising process. The DNA code is a prospective blueprint, which can be deciphered.[3]

Only since the 1950s, when the language of DNA was deciphered, have we known how the complex process of building our body-minds was accomplished. The awesome intelligence at the nucleus of every cell guides embryogenesis from a fertilized egg through birth, maturation, and death. (Rupert Sheldrake's theory of morphic resonance, mentioned earlier, hypothesizes that there is more to it than instructions from DNA — suggesting there may be an invisible field that holds the experience of all members of a species.) And Bruce Lipton, in *The Biology of Belief*, finds that it is the membrane around the cell that holds the cell's intelligence.[4]

One of the critical design innovations for the biosphere and multicellular life was the process of photosynthesis, which occurred hundreds of millions of years ago, and transformed our barren planet into a living biosphere.

The design innovation that allowed the emergence of *Homo sapiens* from the animal world was language, culture, and the ability to communicate exo-genetically — outside the genetic code. In *Science and Sanity* Alfred Korzybski called this ability "time-binding" — the capacity to pass on information to one another through language, symbols, arts, and music.[5] Whereas biological evolution takes millions of years, cultural and social evolution takes place within hundreds of years and now at a faster pace — only decades. Through language, each generation learns from the one before, vastly accelerating the process of change. Language and culture built the noosphere, just as the process of photosynthesis and biological organisms — plants, animals, insects — built the biosphere.

Conscious evolution is the next design innovation. It is based on our ability to understand the innovations of the past, such that we can consciously codesign our future, drawing on the knowledge of how nature formed matter, how DNA intelligence works, how photosynthesis occurs, how ecological systems are maintained, and how language, culture, and technology affect us. Conscious evolution is a natural extension of the ongoing process of evolutionary innovations leading to greater awareness, freedom, and capacity.

The new worldview already exists in an early stage. There is a large and growing body of knowledge in almost every arena — science, psychology, cosmology, art, literature, philosophy, and business. For example, a group of evolutionary leaders (www .evolutionaryleaders.net) have issued a Call to Conscious Evolution. However, there is not yet an established field within the intellectual community called conscious evolution to coordinate all the separate insights. Our fledgling worldview is still almost invisible, yet it is drawing to it brilliant minds in every field and function who hold the mysterious sense of hope for the future.

CHAPTER SIX

Exploring the Meaning of
Conscious Evolution

It is important to realize how radically new the concept of conscious evolution is. As an emerging worldview, it only became more broadly recognized in the 1960s, because the primary conditions that brought it into existence are themselves only that recent. This newness explains why it has not yet been incorporated into our academic, political, and religious worldviews.

There are three new elements vital to conscious evolution. I call them "the three Cs": new cosmology, new crises, and new capacities.

New Cosmology: The First C

Our understanding of cosmogenesis has brought forth a new vision of all creation. In the mid-1960s two scientists, Arno Penzias and Robert Wilson, identified background radiation from the original moment of creation — the big bang — and were able to extrapolate backward in time to those first instants of creation.

"What they were hearing was nothing less than the vibration of the birth of the universe," wrote Richard Elliott Friedman in *The Disappearance of God: A Divine Mystery*.[1]

Theodore B. Roszak wrote in *The Voice of the Earth*:

> The universe has altered radically over time. It has a history. These findings — background radiation, the quasar, the big bang, and later Stephen Hawking's research on black holes — rapidly coalesced with quantum mechanics and Einstein's relativity to produce a radically new world picture. We now know that history is the characteristic of everything, not only living things. We know that the heavier elements we are made of were forged during that history in the deep interior of stars. We know that whatever exists, no matter how intricate, has to be accounted for within the dynamics of cosmic expansion and the framework of cosmic time.[2]

Anyone born before the 1960s was not educated in the crucial new idea that the physical universe had a beginning in time, has been evolving for billions of years, and is still evolving now through us as well as throughout the entire cosmos. When I went to college in the early 1950s, I was told that the frontiers of knowledge had been mostly closed. Neither our new creation story nor the new worldview was even considered at that time.

The importance of the new cosmology is that we recognize the universe has a history and a direction and, therefore, so do we. It reinforces the new story. The metapattern that connects everything is involved not only in living systems but in the entire process of creation. The universe has been evolving in time toward ever-more-complex systems with ever-greater freedom and consciousness. There has been a cosmological phase, from the big bang to the first cell; a biological phase, from the first cell to the first human; a noological phase, from the first human to us.

And now, we are entering a cocreative phase, when human life becomes consciously coevolutionary with nature.

The idea that there is a history to everything is a fundamental component in conscious evolution. It reinforces our desire to evolve in history rather than purely metaphysically, or in another afterworld, yet helps us see the future not as more of the same, but as radically new and self-transcending, fulfilling our deepest aspirations for transformation. It gives us long-range visions not only of our past, billions of years ago, but of our future, which is estimated to continue hundreds of billions of years beyond our lifetimes.

This immense scope of time relieves us from any absolute sense of limitation and gives us hope that in some way our species is becoming more mature and creative, and that we can have an ever-evolving future. We now begin to cultivate a new sense of identity, not as isolated individuals in a meaningless universe, but rather as vehicles through which the universe is evolving. As the universe in person, we cocreate the next stage of our own evolution. We can place our own capacity for conscious innovations in the lineage of past design innovations such as the synthesis of matter, the DNA code, photosynthesis, and language. All of these have led to the new design innovation, conscious evolution.

New Crises: The Second C

Our new crises are another vital element to conscious evolution, especially the environmental crisis. From the perspective of the new story, this complex crisis can be understood as a natural but dangerous stage in the birth process of a universal humanity.

We are undergoing the shift in a planetary "birth" of the next era of evolution. As we have already seen, what worked before will now destroy us. We must rapidly stop doing what we have done so successfully — building, populating, polluting, and using up nonrenewable resources to survive. We did not know that any of this was wrong, dangerous, or self-centered. Now we realize that cataclysms have wiped out whole species: 98 percent of all species became extinct before humans appeared. But never before did a species know ahead of time that it might self-destruct and that it had an option to do something about it. Now we are shifting from reactive response to proactive choice. Our crisis is an evolutionary driver awakening us to the necessity and opportunity to choose a future commensurate with our potential and to take responsibility for our actions.

I believe that collectively, we do know how to coordinate ourselves as a whole, how to handle our waste, shift to renewable resources, and awaken to our unique, new roles in the maturation of our species. If the crisis is natural, so is the response.

The newness of the crisis means, however, that no existing leaders or institutions in the current top-down political, religious, and corporate structures can train us. No team is waiting at the end of the birth canal, as far as we know! The process of awakening comes from our deeper and more intuitive knowing combined with scientific understanding. This is why I call us Generation One, the first on this Earth to face evolution or extinction as a species together.

New Capacities: The Third C

Our new capacities — powers now available to us, such as biotechnology, nuclear power, nanotechnology, cybernetics, artificial intelligence, artificial life, and space development — are radical evolutionary capacities that are potentially dangerous in our current state of self-centered consciousness. From our present perspective they may seem unnatural, and indeed they are. Yet, if we consider our needs at the next stage of evolution — as a universal species — these may be precisely the abilities we require to survive and grow in the extended physical environment of outer space, and in the expanded consciousness environment of inner space.

In a biological organism, for example, capacities that are lethal in the womb are vital in the world. So our extraordinary new powers, which can be deadly to us in our current stage of self-centeredness and planet-boundedness, may be natural for us at the next stage of cosmic consciousness and universal life.

Because we fear the danger of misusing our new technologies in the present, we must not prematurely destroy them. Rather, we should see ahead to their possible use at the next stage of evolution and guide their application toward the emancipation of our evolutionary potential rather than attempting the impossible task of stopping knowledge and preserving the status quo. We must remember that the nature of nature is to transform — especially when nature hits a crisis of limits.

From the perspective of the three Cs, we can see that the new cosmology can be interpreted as the story of the birth of a universal humanity, that our new crises are the results of our natural evolutionary process, and that our new capacities are the growing powers of a young, universal species — all barely one generation old.

Learning Conscious Evolution

How do we become conscious of conscious evolution? How does the new worldview penetrate the essence of our being and animate our actions? The key assumption here is that there is a natural pattern for the development of a planetary system, just as there is for a biological system. This pattern resides in the integration of the fields of knowing — spiritual, social, and scientific/technological. Something novel is possible when these fields become a new, whole system, different from and greater than the sum of its parts.

1. SPIRITUAL CONSCIOUS EVOLUTION

The spiritual aspect of conscious evolution gives us access to that deeper pattern within us. We become conscious of the evolutionary impulse — the dynamic process of creation — through inner guidance, motivation, intuition, and revelation. It is the feeling within us urging us to be more, to know more, to love more, to reach out and touch, to activate our genius, to find our life purpose. It is Spirit in action, God in evolution, the consciousness force, cosmic intelligence, the supramental genius of the universe, or whatever name we choose. (There is currently no agreed-upon word for the evolutionary aspect of God or Spirit.)

In conscious evolution, our spiritual experience expands to include resonance with the design of evolution. We incarnate the impulse of evolution as our own inner motivation to be more of who we truly are. The process of creation itself is incarnating in a new way as we become more creative. In spiritual terms, God is creating "godlings." The Creator is creating cocreators. Spirit is creating "con-spiritors."

Our spiritual growth awakens our social potential, pressing us deeper inward to pick up that design and outward to express our creativity in the world through our unique vocation. We work from within ourselves toward higher consciousness, greater freedom, and more complex order to effect a change in the world, first and foremost through our personal evolution.

With conscious evolution we develop an expanded spirituality — an *evolutionary* spirituality — as we learn to attune to the inner patterns of creation that are oriented toward higher consciousness, freedom, and more complex order. The lives of great avatars were transformed by oneness with this deeper reality. Now, because of the rise of consciousness in ourselves, our lives are also lifted up, not as saints or seers, but as humans at the next stage of our natural evolution — cocreative with the processes of evolution. This is not a slight improvement, but rather a species metamorphosis.

In *Design for Evolution*, Erich Jantsch coined a beautiful word to describe this expanding form of spiritual awareness: "syntony." He compared syntony to a way of knowing through resonance, or harmonizing with that which we seek to know. Jantsch wrote:

> Syntony, which seems to be due to direct communication of individual human consciousness through some resonance process, seems to exhibit the same characteristics of holographic communication that seem to govern genetic information and brain functions. ... As we have learned, though not too well, to design social roles, we shall have to learn now to design systems of syntony; this implies a shift of focus from the rational level through the mythological to the evolutionary level of inquiry.[3]

In summary, the first way of accessing conscious evolution is to deliberately cultivate the capacity for inner knowing — syntony — spiritual resonance with the patterns of creation. We use our innate abilities to receive intuition, to act upon it, to accept feedback from the outside world, receiving further guidance, reaching out to test the guidance again and again until we learn to act spontaneously and directly from whole-system intelligence.

2. SOCIAL CONSCIOUS EVOLUTION

As we gain deeper alignment with the patterns of creation, we see a suffering world that is out of alignment. We see systems that are breaking down, causing misery, alienation, and violence almost everywhere. This breakdown is natural from the point of view that we are undergoing an evolutionary shift. Crises precede transformation.

Through conscious evolution we realize, for the first time

as a species, that it is our responsibility to proactively design social systems that are in alignment with the tendency in nature toward higher consciousness, greater freedom, and more synergistic order. With our increase in freedom because of our new powers comes a commensurate increase in responsibility for the use of those powers. We no longer accept our society and its ills as a given; we become proactive, social cocreators and the social potential movement awakens. Not only a few outstanding social activists or leaders participate, but millions of so-called ordinary people in myriad organizations, projects, and initiatives undertake the work of healing and evolving our world.

For example, we need a sustainable, regenerative economy and monetary system that take into account that we are one planetary system in which we are all vital members, integrated in an environment that is part of our body, in a social system that frees us to express our life purpose in creative work.

We need a new, universally available health care system that reinforces responsibility, self-healing, and, eventually, increased longevity and life-extension. We need mature media that communicate growth potential and the *new* news of our innovations and successes. We need a new form of self-governance that truly involves all of us in a deeper responsibility for ourselves and others, a genuine "higher-self" governance. It would be a form of governance that cultivates social synergy, supporting us in seeking common goals and matching needs with resources in the light of our full potential.

The purpose of this book is not to outline the next step of evolution, but only to place these needed changes in the context of the new worldview and reality of our own capacity for conscious evolution. These changes, and far more, are all parts of the enormous task of the social potential movement, yet we are blessed with the resources and intelligence to do it because so many of us have started to live our life purpose and desire to express our creativity in the world. And, due in part to the rapid maturation of social media of all kinds, we can accelerate our self- and social evolution by connecting the best innovations that embody humanity's evolutionary potential.

As the spiritual aspect of conscious evolution requires the deepening of our inner sensitivity to the patterns of creation, so the social aspect requires us to learn how to form cooperative and interconnected social systems into which we can enter as individuals and sense that we are a vital and loving part of a whole. Rather than addressing this question from the outside — as changes that must be made in society "out there" — the social potential movement attempts to discover the synergistic, win-win social patterns from the inside. This discovery is made through integration of our body, mind, and spirit, through spiritual attunement with the patterns that connect, through our intimate relationships with one another, through learning how to relate as partners rather than as dominators, through understanding and aligning with ecological and biological natural systems, and through discovering and committing to fulfilling our vocations. New social designs come forth from compassion and our deeper understanding of nature, human nature, and systems in resonance with the patterns in the process of creation, as described extensively in Hazel Henderson's book *Building a Win-Win World* and in the work of Elisabet Sahtouris. In her article "The Biology of Globalization," Sahtouris writes, "The globalization of humanity is a natural, biological, evolutionary process. Yet we face an enormous crisis, because the most central and important aspect of globalization, its economy, is currently being organized in a manner that so gravely violates the fundamental principles by which healthy living systems are organized that it threatens the demise of our whole civilization."[4]

Perhaps it is a matter of timing. It was not possible to create harmonious societies at any large scale, beyond the relatively peaceful tribal cultures, until the events of the last decades — the period of our birth — just as it is not possible for a fetus to get up and walk. Perhaps the great visions of new societies could not have been realized until we passed through the events we are still undergoing, which include:

- the maturation of the noosphere, which gives us the technical and communication capacities to connect globally, and at the speed of light, via cell phones, all social media, and the internet, along with the social capacity, in some parts of the world, to produce in abundance, to prolong our lives, to live in freedom, to be educated, to have mobility, and to have free choice of vocation;
- the relatively new widespread access to education through trainings, teachings, seminars, internet courses, and mystic and mystery schools that provide the kind of learning opportunities that once were only available to a few;
- the awakening of a critical mass of evolving humans, able to attune to the processes of evolution within themselves, moving from self-centered toward whole-centered consciousness, free to find life purpose and creative action;
- reaching the limits to growth on a finite planet, learning how to shift to renewable, clean, and, eventually, fully abundant resources and energy, whether through a hydrogen economy, solar energy from space, free energy from the vacuum field, zero point energy, or other possibilities;
- the shift from procreation to cocreation, freeing the creativity of women from the enormous task of maximum reproduction to give their loving energy to chosen children and to the larger human family, while liberating men from the burden of feeding and protecting large families.

Perhaps the utopian visions of a new heaven and a new Earth that have arisen for hundreds if not thousands of years are accurate precognitions of coming evolutionary possibilities. Perhaps these visions could not come true until we matured to the next stage of our evolution, the process we are undergoing now.

We have been young *Homo sapiens*, the big-brained creature that knows it knows, with an immortal spirit in a degenerating body, living in environments of scarcity, working ceaselessly to survive, and dying young. Now we are on the verge of becoming a universal humanity — cocreators, capable of producing abundance for all in a universal environment with extended life spans and greater opportunity for individual expression. The actualization of these social visions has required the maturation of humanity to the stage of conscious evolution.

3. Scientific and Technological Conscious Evolution

Through molecular biology, nanotechnology, artificial intelligence, robotics, astronautics, and genetics, combined with the noetic science of consciousness, we are shifting from matter-dominance to life-dominance. Our collective human intelligence is penetrating the invisible veil of nature to understand nature's processes and technologies of creation. As we understand the nature of matter as energy and information in motion, we become less dominated by it and more able to influence matter consciously.

Each scientist and technologist is part of a vast invisible web of hundreds of thousands of others, all drawing on the shared noosphere built by the genius of the past and by those in the present who are working in countless laboratories around the globe. Every advance made in the world is quickly communicated to other parts of the world. Through this collective capacity we are consciously entering the process of nature. We have taken a step toward Chaisson's "Life Era," in which technologically competent humans are gaining an understanding of matter, thereby changing the nature of evolution itself. Instead of seeing technology as merely useful or possibly destructive, we see it as the natural extension of nature's technologies, giving human nature the capacity to evolve evolution itself from unconscious to conscious choice.

Making a good synthesis, Jerry Glenn wrote:

> In this worldview we are seeking the merger of the mystic and the technocrat to achieve an altogether new civilization. When this happens in the 21st century we will have a world renaissance that could be properly called the "Conscious Technological Civilization..." There will be many views of the mutual creation of consciousness and technology, but the core view will be determined by the future relationship of the "mystics" or the masters of consciousness and the "technocrat" or the masters of technology...it is possible to merge such different world views, if the merger is with the mystics' attitude toward the world and the technocrats' knowledge of the world.[5]

As Nassim Haramein, founder of the Resonance Project, told me in a personal conversation, we will not need to manipulate our own biology, but rather tap into the causal level in the quantum vacuum. We will be able to "engineer the vacuum," as Haramein puts it. We will thus gain direct access to the almost infinite energy in the vacuum. We will gain the capacity to affect gravity and to evolve our own bodies, eventually transcending the current creature-human condition through resonance with geometric structures at the causal level, that which is causing physics and biology. We are midway between the infinitely large and infinitely small, capable of resonating with the fundamental code of evolution.[6]

Now that we are learning to evolve consciously, we must learn to apply values to guide the use of these tremendous new capacities in science and technology — along with all other disciplines. If we accept an evolutionary agenda as the overarching goal in this millennium, then our scientific and technological brilliance will be naturally guided in that direction. We must learn to value scientific innovations crucial to nonlinear, quantum progress. For example, we know that solar energy will be a major energy resource within the next hundred years. This may lead to an economy based on hydrogen as the delivery system for all clean energies.

To allow for scientific and technological genius to fully come forth, certain systems will have to dramatically change. For example, the military-technological-industrial complex will have to be transformed, either by collapse or by the evolution of civilization. I believe that if and when we choose to develop truly evolutionary social and technological goals — such as new worlds in the human mind, new worlds on Earth, and new worlds in space — we will find that we will have undertaken a global mission of such excitement and greatness that it will attract people to participate. This whole-system societal shift will call forth the military-industrial complex to fulfill its own magnificent destiny to build new worlds on Earth and in space for a universal humanity, and eventually new species and new worlds.

Society has not broadly supported such design innovations because of its short-term, consumption-based, and profit-based mentality. We must begin to see the depth and breadth of our unborn history and let the self-evident lessons of evolution proactively guide our new scientific and technological genius. Eventually, this genius will be called forth to join in the evolutionary process itself as we learn to become a solar-system species and even a galactic species in a universe of billions of other Earth-sized planets.

Science and technology, however, cannot establish its goals

alone, any more than the military or economic sectors can. It is only through the full-scale activation of a social potential movement that humans will be able to fully evolve spiritually, politically, scientifically, and technologically. This is a whole-system change, and to activate it we will have to develop whole-system structures and models into which to transform, as described in chapter 11.

If we can learn to combine our advanced technological capacities with an evolved spirituality and the ability to design synergistic social systems and sustainable, nonpolluting technologies, we will be part of a quantum transformation, a jump as great as the jump from Neanderthal to *Homo sapiens*. Conscious evolution is the design innovation that empowers us to become a universal humanity. We are crossing the evolutionary divide between creature and cocreator.

CHAPTER SEVEN

The Fabric of Civilization

Conscious evolution is the new worldview vital to ethical evolution. It is a meme to guide us through this dangerous period toward an unlimited future. Memes are ideas woven into complex thought systems that organize human activities according to a specific pattern. The way genes build bodies, memes build cultures, societies, and the noosphere.

The word "meme," as we are defining it here, was coined by evolutionary biologist Richard Dawkins in his book *The Selfish Gene*.[1] Howard Bloom beautifully described memes in his book *The Lucifer Principle*:

> The meme is a self-replicating cluster of ideas. Thanks
> to a handful of biological tricks, these visions become the
> glue that holds together civilizations, giving each culture
> its distinctive shape. Genes sit at the center of each cellular
> blob, dictating the construction of a multi-billion-celled
> body like yours and mine. As genes are to the organism,

so memes are to the super-organism — the noosphere — pulling together millions of individuals into a collective creature of awesome size. Memes stretch their tendrils through the fabric of each human brain, driving us to coagulate in the cooperative masses of family, tribe, and nation.[2]

Memes and Society

Memes are the most powerful force in human society. They guide our actions, build our societies, and organize our world. Just as genes are selected based on their ability to survive, so too memes are selected for their viability.

In recent history we have seen certain deadly memes gain enormous power, then disintegrate almost completely. For example, Nazism was a vicious meme that gripped the German people, stimulating them to commit acts that are unthinkable to virtually all Germans now. Daniel Jonah Goldhagen wrote in *Hitler's Willing Executioners: Ordinary Germans and the Holocaust*, "Germany during the Nazi period was inhabited by people animated by beliefs about Jews that made them willing to become consenting mass executioners...."[3] When the Nazis were defeated, that meme dissolved (or became recessive, since it still festers under the surface like a virus ready to infect the social memetic code). People changed their behavior, radically. Modern German society cannot conceive of burning, torturing, enslaving, starving, or exterminating millions of people.

The German people were not intrinsically mass murderers — they were taken over by a diabolic meme that was created out of a sinister and deliberate mixture of myth, fear, and power. This reason does not excuse or justify, for ultimately we are responsible for the memes we allow to guide us. The problem is, we usually don't know we have a meme, or rather, that a meme has us. Typically, we accept the consensual worldview without even noticing it. Conscious evolution teaches us to be meme conscious and create life-affirming memes that foster a positive future.

Communism was another recent worldview, or memetic code, that directed the energies and actions of millions for nearly a century. Karl Marx and Friedrich Engels's economic philosophy was adapted by Lenin and the Bolsheviks, who eventually destroyed whole classes of people in the name of an ideal of a new society. Like Nazism, Communism, although born of what some people believed was an ideal, proved to be a lethal meme. It did not take into account human freedom and dignity, and it undermined the moral, spiritual, and productive capacities of a great people.

Another meme, that of "mutually assured destruction" combined with thermonuclear war, was designed by the United States and the Soviet Union as a defense strategy.

While memes can be used harmfully, they can also be vital agents of change! The meme of conscious evolution, given modern communications, could and indeed must spread very quickly. Within a few decades it could become the guiding meme for a cocreative future. Howard Bloom wrote in *The Lucifer Principle*, "The meme of Christianity restructured the Roman Empire a mere 300 years after Jesus completed his Sermon on the Mount. Similarly, Marxism radically altered the shape of Russian society a startling 60 years after Karl [Marx] the cantankerous ambled out of the British Museum's library with the final manuscript of *Das Kapital* tucked tightly under his arm."[4]

When a meme no longer seems to explain the nature of reality or guides us toward goals that satisfy our deepest desires, it recedes or quickly becomes extinct. For example, prior to Gorbachev's glasnost and perestroika that started in the mid-1980s, Communists proclaimed that their ideology was the best in the world. By 1990 it was difficult to find anyone who believed in that authoritarian system. Former proponents denounced the dying meme, claiming they always knew it was wrong, just as Germans denounced Nazism.

Now that the meme of Communism has disintegrated, people who had been controlled by it are confused and disoriented, often returning to authoritarian models of the past. Liberal democracy is an alien meme to them and tends to be rejected, much like a transplanted organ in the human body is often rejected. When healthy memes don't exist, however, recessive memes can resurface and take over, such as extreme nationalism or racial and ethnic hatred. It is very dangerous for a culture to be without a healthy meme.

The demise of Nazism and Communism has forced us to look at our own situation. Some of the most precious memes in the Western world are fading rapidly. Their passing has left us seemingly without shared values and a common awareness of life purpose. For example, the story told in the Bible is no longer *literally* believable for millions. The worldview, or meme, of biblical literalism is dissolving in light of both scientific and historical research. Cosmologists know the world was not built in seven days. Historical scholars assert that Jesus said only a fraction of the adages in the Gospels. Scriptural narratives contradict one another and may not be based on historical fact but on faith, myth, and mystery. According to some scholars, the Gospels are a collection of great stories, insights, and spiritual truths compiled by a community of Jewish people inspired by one man of extraordinary, godlike qualities. Bishop John Shelby Spong suggested in *Liberating the Gospels* that these people attempted to tell the story of his life in such a way as to conform to Jewish scripture and prophesy.[5] Whatever the historical facts may be, it is increasingly difficult for many people to believe the stories exactly as they were written. Although a spiritual understanding of scripture is deepening in many, the undermining of the Bible's picture of reality and its ignorance of cosmogenesis is deconstructing the dogmas of the Western world. For example, in her books *The Emergent Christ* and *Christ in Evolution,* Catholic scholar Ilia Delio reimagines Christianity from an evolutionary perspective.[6]

In the same way that Christianity is evolving, so science itself is required to mature under the impetus of its own magnificent intelligence. Scientific materialism was the meme that displaced biblical literalism. But even the memes that describe matter, eternal time, and random chance, the basis of the scientific worldview, no longer fit all the facts as revealed by scientific investigation. Matter has been dematerialized to the point of taking on certain attributes of mind. Eternal time has given way to duration and the directional unfolding of evolution in specific time frames, and chance could not be responsible for the complex order in the universe given the fact that there is no eternal time. For example, it seems incredible, statistically, that the universe could have been organized to its current degree of complexity in only 13.8 billion years. Theodore Roszak wrote in *The Voice of the Earth*:

> In the late 1970s Fred Hoyle and Chandra Wickrama-singhe calculated the odds that life could have originated from just such an undirected sloshing about. Rather than trying to compute the probability for an entire organism springing into existence, they limited the problem to a sequence of twenty or thirty key amino acids in the enzymes of some hypothetical cell. The number they came up with was one chance in 1,040,000.[7]

Ken Wilber wrote in *A Brief History of Everything*, "Something more than chance is pushing the universe. For traditional scientists, chance was their salvation. Chance would explain all. Chance, plus unending time would produce the universe. But they don't have unending time, and so their god fails them miserably.

That god is dead. Chance is not what explains the universe; in fact, chance is exactly what the self-transcending drive of the Kosmos overcomes."[8]

The meme of individualistic democracy, although still the best of all existing systems of governance, is incomplete as a guiding idea. In the United States, we need only to look at our streets, jails, homeless shelters, and paralyzed Congress to see the results of a form of democracy rife with individualism, competition, and corporate control in a commercialized world. Arthur Schlesinger described it as the "disuniting of America," as ethnic, religious, sexual, racial, and other special interest groups fortify themselves by putting others down.[9] Most especially, we see the loss of community, the breakup of the family, and the alienation and self-destructive violence among the young. The meme of secular, liberal democracy is good, but not sufficient. Reactionary or conservative response, however, is not the answer. Although conservatism is an effort to reaffirm personal responsibility and creativity, it lacks a new vision and a new social architecture to foster both cooperation and responsibility.

Our goal cannot be to return to the past, nor can it be to move forward to a future that is more of the same. A vast array of positive social innovations leading to reintegration of community, participatory management, and economic reforms is now helping us work toward a new level of cooperation and community. The full expression of this emerging leadership is not possible in the political realm, however, until we have a new context in which to see our possibilities and an idea of where we are leading ourselves. To lead means we are going somewhere. Without this new awareness, we cannot lead, maintain, or improve the status quo — whether on the right, left, or center. We have entered a "chaos point" that cannot be maintained.

As Ervin Laszlo wrote in his book *Chaos Point 2012 and Beyond*,

"A chaos point is the crucial tipping point in the evolution of a system in which trends that have brought the system to its present state break down and it can no longer return to its prior states and modes of behavior: it is launched irreversibly on a new trajectory that leads either to breakdown or to breakthrough to a new structure and a new mode of operation."[10]

When we understand our evolutionary potential, however, and awaken to our emerging social, spiritual, and scientific capacities to fulfill an evolutionary agenda, new leadership can and already is beginning to cocreate and consciously choose the memes needed to empower it. Society will be activated with excitement and hope as creative possibilities call forth the potential of millions.

The meme of profit-centered, self-centered capitalism also fails as a worldview to guide us into the twenty-first century. We see the spread of poverty, damage to the environment, and massive power in the hands of ever fewer individuals and global corporations. Paul Hawken wrote in *The Ecology of Commerce*, "Like a sunset effect, the glories of industrial capitalism may mask the fact that it is poised at a declining horizon of options and possibilities. Just as internal contradictions brought down the Marxist and socialist economies, so do a different set of social and biological forces signal our own possible demise."[11]

The current economic system is not sustainable. According to Hawken, we are involved in a slow-motion holocaust to our life-support system. If we do not recognize that every business, corporation, or enterprise is part of the whole system, and must take feedback from the whole system, and be accountable for its effect on the environment, we cannot continue to evolve, or even survive. Billionaire financier George Soros wrote in the *Atlantic Monthly*, February 1997, "Although I have made a fortune in the financial markets, I now fear that the untrammeled intensification of laissez-faire capitalism and the spread of market values into all areas of life is endangering our open and democratic society. The main enemy of the open society, I believe, is no longer the communist but the capitalist threat."[12]

The Importance of Memes

In the past, memes arose unconsciously and directed our actions, often without our knowing consent. But now, not only are we responsible for our actions, but we are also responsible for our beliefs. For as we see reality, so we act, and as we act, so we shape reality. All ideas are human made, and none are the absolute truth. Common sense dictates that we evaluate our beliefs on the basis of how they affect us. If they make us more loving, creative, and wise, they are good beliefs. If they make us cruel, jealous, depressed, and sick, they cannot be good beliefs or memes.

For example, I tried in my early years to be what I thought was an existentialist. It was in Paris before I met my husband. I smoked Gauloises, drank red wine, and tried to believe in the meaninglessness of the universe and of myself. I became more despairing. Later, in the 1950s when my husband and I went to parties in New York, I occasionally expressed a naive sense of hope — that something magnificent was to come from the human enterprise. The artists, poets, and playwrights of that time, imbued with an existentialist, or even a nihilistic, worldview scorned me and sent me home in tears! I became determined to find out what I was hopeful about! I searched through literature seeking clues to discover a new image of humanity, a new meme that not only seemed true, but was also scientifically sound and would correspond with my intuitive sense of meaning and hope. In the 1960s I discovered the ideas of such evolutionary thinkers as Teilhard de Chardin, Sri Aurobindo and his partner the Mother, Abraham H. Maslow, Buckminster Fuller, Lancelot Law Whyte, Peter Russell, Margaret Mead, Ruth Benedict, and Jonas Salk, which changed my beliefs and transformed my life.

I was exhilarated and motivated to seek my vocation in the world. I wrote and published the "Center Letter," a first networking letter to more than one thousand leaders at the frontier of change, asking them what they thought was the next step for the future good. I called people I admired, like Maslow, and invited them to lunch. Maslow gave me three hundred names of his "Eupsychian network" to write to.

I will never forget the day I met Jonas Salk. I had written a letter to Jerry Piel, president of *Scientific American* magazine, describing my ideas of a "theater of man," which I heard Salk wanted to build at the newly forming Salk Institute. Salk read the letter, called me, and said we were "two peas in the same evolutionary pod." In September 1964 he invited me to lunch. He was the first truly evolutionary soul I encountered. Conscious evolution was the theme of his life. I shared with him all the ideas I had gleaned from my reading and then told him what was "wrong" with me — my love of the future and my desire to connect with everything. He smiled and said, "Barbara, these are not faults. These are exactly the characteristics needed by evolution. You are a mutant." Salk introduced me to others who shared my perspective. I met Louis Kahn, the architect who was building the Salk Institute; Al Rosenfeld, science editor of *Life* magazine; and others. Suddenly the strange and somewhat lost person I had been grew into a highly motivated futurist and social innovator. I wrote in my (unpublished) journal, Christmas 1964:

> The problem of identity has disappeared. I can never again say, as I once did, "in my own eyes I am nothing," for as all people are, I too am the inheritor of the evolution of the ages. In my genes are the generations. Every cell in my body identifies me with the great and terrible adventure of inanimate to animate to human, and every desire of my being sets me passionately to work to further the rise of humaneness out of humanity. I am what was

and what will be. If I am nothing, life is nothing; that it cannot be — and be.

Through the ideas and the affirmation of kindred souls, all imbued with the new meme of conscious evolution, my life transformed and I set upon the ever-evolving evolutionary journey. The new meme, and meeting several people conscious of this potential who could also see it awakening in me, transformed my life. As we awaken to the full scope of what it means to incarnate the impulse of evolution, it is vital that we help each other recognize the qualities of our emerging potential so that we can each believe in and live our own genuine possibility. It is so important to be seen for who we truly are.

In his seminal book, *Science and Sanity* Alfred Korzybski, whose work helped found the field of general semantics, made the point that the map is not the territory.[13] The word is not the thing, just as the belief about reality is not reality itself. We become conscious that we are abstracting from a vast nonverbal event through our nervous systems. This abstraction reaches our brains and becomes meaningful to us through our personal worldview — through the image of reality that we hold. People with different pictures of reality see events differently and therefore act differently. Our worldview is important. It profoundly shapes how we see reality and how we act.

As David L. Cooperrider writes in *Appreciative Management and Leadership: The Power of Positive Thought and Action in Organizations*, "to a far greater extent than is normally acknowledged, we human beings create our own realities through symbolic and mental processes and that because of this conscious evolution of the future is a human option."[14]

I can think of no finer lens to see the world through than conscious evolution. It expands our horizon to see humanity moving toward a higher dimension of life itself. I believe that conscious evolution is the emerging meme needed to guide us toward a more just, humane, and regenerative world.

The effort to develop a new meme is a vital aspect of feeding the hungry, healing the sick, stopping the violence, and freeing the world of poisonous toxins. We are seeking here to piece together a new memetic code equal to our spiritual, social, and scientific potential, in alignment with the process of evolution itself. The most direct path to our survival and fulfillment is to develop and communicate an idea system that guides us toward ethical evolution.

CHAPTER EIGHT

Embracing Conscious Evolution

A s we have seen, conscious evolution is a "mother" meme, calling together individual memes that hold information for creating new communications, arts, sciences, education, business, environmental organizations, and health systems — the new social body. Conscious evolution encourages all groups to come together and compose a great and magnificent matrix in which to flourish — a new memetic code for the emerging social body. Our mother meme provides a magnetic field for this momentous gathering. We might call our new memetic code the chrysalis in which the butterfly self-assembles.

The Fulfillment of Human Endeavor

Conscious evolution calls upon scientists and technologists to help us understand the laws and recurring patterns in the evolutionary process. This understanding will guide us in designing and using new technologies for our evolutionary agenda, the ethical evolution of ourselves toward universal life — the next turn in the Evolutionary Spiral.

Conscious evolution calls upon political leaders to move us toward a synergistic democracy that considers each of us as creative members of the whole community and ecology. We need to be guided toward the next stage of individualism. The success of modern society has led to new problems: the separation of individuals from one another, from their families, from their communities, and now from their jobs, as corporations downsize and all allegiances dissolve in the quest for survival and concern for the bottom line. Conscious evolution sets the stage for the next phase of individualism wherein we seek our uniqueness not through separation but through deeper participation in the whole.

Except for great individuals like Lincoln, Gandhi, Gorbachev, the Dalai Lama, Nelson Mandela, most so-called political leaders find it almost impossible to guide genuine change. The higher they get toward the top of pyramidal systems, the less power they appear to have to change anything. That's in part because real power to change lies with those in every field joining to cocreate a better design of social systems. Real power to change happens when we connect what is working and empower one another to be the change we all want to see in the world. Current governmental leaders will become most effective when they become facilitators of these new initiatives for people everywhere, rather than leaders in the old way.

Conscious evolution needs evolutionary artists to tell the new stories of our collective potential in a variety of ways. Without vision, the people perish. With vision, we flourish. Currently we are in the catacombs, like early Christians, scratching pictures on the walls of caves as we communicate through journals, conferences, lectures, seminars, books, blogs, and emails. We encourage new forms of theater, music, dance, novels, poetry, and films

— participatory art forms that can inspire and lift our vision to help us see ourselves as participants in the great human drama of creation. Evolutionary artists are needed to bring our new story of creation to life, much like the great Greek playwrights, sculptors, and architects did for the Homeric stories; the geniuses of the Middle Ages did to illuminate the Gospels; and those of the Renaissance did to bring the individual human alive and visible upon the stage of history.

Conscious evolution is now calling forth humanistic, transpersonal, spiritual, and evolutionary psychologies to move us from the early phase of personal growth and self-empowerment to the later stages of self-realization and self-actualization through chosen work that is intrinsically self-rewarding. Maslow first outlined these ideas when he described the self-actualizing person. Self-actualization is a process of deep engagement through expressing life's purpose. Now there is much more emphasis on positive psychology and self-actualization in psychology than when Maslow first started his work.

For example, in his seminal book, *Flow: The Psychology of Optimal Experience*, Mihaly Csikszentmihalyi outlines his theory that people are happiest when they are in a state of *flow*.[1] In an interview with *Wired* magazine, Csikszentmihalyi described flow as "being completely involved in an activity for its own sake. The ego falls away. Time flies. Every action, movement, and thought follows inevitably from the previous one, like playing jazz. Your whole being is involved, and you're using your skills to the utmost."[2]

Reading this description of flow reminds me of what happens when people get turned on by conscious evolution and allow themselves to fully engage their unique passion and creative potential in the world. Psychology is studying such states and helping us understand how to access them.

Conscious evolution also calls for educators to take the overview perspective on evolutionary history as a whole process of creation, called Big History, and place ourselves in that history as participants in it. This perspective offers the whole view of evolutionary history from deep time past into deep time present toward deep time future. It also encourages participants to find their natural creative callings within the various functions of the evolving world, including health, environment, education, governance, and other sectors of society.

In this new design for evolutionary education, a metadiscipline is beginning to arise in which teachers and students join together and create a new holistic intellectual basis for transformative education. Such a basis leads us from the confusion of the modern world to the fulfillment of the evolutionary agenda — freeing ourselves from hunger, disease, ignorance, and war — and activating human creativity and the universal future awaiting us. We need educators to help our children understand that they are a treasure and that education is a treasure hunt to help them find their unique genius, which can then be used where it is most needed in the emerging world.

As we begin consciously evolving, the political system will have to respond. As a new, more responsive political system emerges, we will demand that our politicians call upon the military genius to help us learn how to shift from weaponry to "livingry," as Buckminster Fuller poetically declared. We need to reorient our extraordinary organizational and technical capacities to restore our environment, protect us from natural disasters and terrorists, and develop peace-building and conflict-resolution skills while we explore and develop our extended environment in outer space. From the evolutionary perspective, we don't reject military or industrial genius, but rather call forth that genius for its new functions — genuine security and greater freedom to express our higher potentials.

In so doing, we honor that our military includes genuine heroes with extraordinary capabilities. My son Lloyd graduated from the Air Force as a lieutenant colonel. He said to me, "Mom, if we could combine your ideas with our excellence, we could get anything done!" Lloyd was right about military excellence. It is up to society as a whole to take charge and call our own military technological genius to its true heroic purposes of excellence and sacrifice for the future of humanity.

Conscious evolution calls on businesses and entrepreneurs to apply their genius to the development of socially responsible business and investment. The goal is a sustainable, regenerative economy that supports restoration of the environment, preservation of species, and the enhancement of human creativity and community, including expanded ownership, network marketing, community-based currencies, microcredit loans, and other such innovations.

Conscious evolution is the context for a "meta-*religio*," a new ground of the whole, calling upon spiritual leaders and practitioners of all faiths to create what Bishop William Swing, retired Episcopal bishop of California, calls a "United Religions" to end the conflict among religions and to bring together the unique gifts of the faiths for the future of humanity. We need to move beyond ecumenical understanding to evolutionary fulfillment through the embodiment of the principles and practices of the great faiths.

Many of us long not for a new religion, but for the evolution of religion, such that we embody the qualities of our master teachers and become conscious cocreators with the divine universal intelligence ourselves. There is now arising a new synthesis called "evolutionary spirituality," pioneered by such leaders as Ken Wilber, Ilia Delio, Beatrice Bruteau, Michael Dowd, John Haught, Craig Hamilton, Andrew Cohen, and Jean Houston. It is science based, often inspired by Teilhard de Chardin and the new story of cosmogenesis.

In evolutionary spirituality, we consciously embody within us the Impulse of Creation as our own motivation to evolve. We realize that we are incarnating the ever-unfolding universe story itself. We are the universe in person, becoming more fully who we can be. This yearning for more is the essence of the impulse of evolution within us.

Evolutionary spirituality springs from "evolutionary consciousness." This can be defined by the "Three Es." The first E is the Eternal — the One, the Source of all being, consciousness. The second E is embodiment. We each embody the whole story of creation in every atom, molecule, and cell. The third E is emergence. It describes the fact that each of us *is* evolution embodying the mysterious process of creation continuing to emerge through us, felt as our own motivation to grow and express new potentials.

My friend Sidney Lanier has written stirring words in *The Sovereign Person*:

> Conscious evolution is a meta-religio for the 21st century. As yet it is undefined and casts an evocative shadow over the mental inscape of all of us in these days. We know something is over: an era or simply the nightmare that has terrified many of us into awareness, simple human maturity. This meta-religio is the headlong convergence of science with the core realizations of the major world religions. Its constituency is the universal sovereign persons — awakened ones — all those who stand free of the old divisive social forms, however noble their past history. We are called to come together in an open and level place with no boundaries, a space in consciousness where we are enfolded within the transcendent community of the universal person, the sacred precincts of the cosmos itself, our temple and home.[3]

Innovators and creators in these and many more fields of human endeavor and thought are already creating vital new memes and are taking action based on these new ideas. When we piece together the picture of what is already happening, we will see the design emerge — the awakening of the social potential movement.

The Mystery of Evolution

The mystery of the process of creation is profound. Whether one believes that the process occurs through basic laws of natural selection and random mutation or one sees a divine design guiding the process — mind in the cosmos, God in the form of a deity or an eternal animating force — the mystery is equally great. Whatever our beliefs, whatever our metaphysical preferences, we are all confronted with a sense of awe and reverence at the exquisite balance of nature, the precise workings of biological organisms, the wonder of the billions of galaxies and the equally infinite fields of subatomic physics where matter disappears and only probabilities exist in a vacuum that may indeed hold the memory of the whole process of creation.

Within this mystery I have perceived some insights that are evolving as understanding grows:

- A designing, creative intelligence animates the universe. It is symbolized by the core running through the Evolutionary Spiral, representing the impulse of evolution. As we mature on a personal and spiritual level, this intelligence becomes personal and conscious through us. God, the creative force of the universe, becomes person as us, yet is never subsumed or limited by us. When we look at the intelligence of the whole system — the design of every atom, molecule, and cell — the experience is that there is a consciousness that transcends its parts, is immanent within them, yet is more than those parts.

- The hypothesis out of which conscious evolution arises is that there exists a universal intelligence that informs the entire evolutionary process — a process that resides in part within the human psyche. In conscious evolution humanity remembers its past as well as its potential future, just as the genetic code of a biological organism holds the memory of its past and provides the design for its potential, yet not predetermined future. As Professor A. Harris Stone wrote in a personal correspondence, "Conscious evolution can be seen as an awakening of the 'memory' that resides in a synthesis of human knowing — spiritual, social, and scientific — joined in the effort to discover the inherent evolutionary design, a design which we strive to manifest through ethical choice and creative action."[4]

- There is both an eternal and an evolving aspect of reality. The eternal is the nonphysical, nonlocal, ineffable "field of all possibilities," as Deepak Chopra called it in his book *The Seven Spiritual Laws of Success*.[5] It is pure consciousness experienced by us subjectively in nondual union with Source or Spirit through meditation, yoga, and other spiritual or mystical experiences.

- The evolving aspect of the transcendent occurs when the unmanifest manifests in form. It resides in the implicate order. The timeless unfolds as duration. In evolution, the One becomes the many. Yet in each of the many resides the One. Each of us reflects both the eternal and the evolving aspects of the universal intelligence. Mystical experience of the past emphasized the eternal aspect of reality. As we enter the age of conscious evolution, however, we become more sensitive to the evolving aspect. We feel it as our motivation to grow, to know, to cocreate a new world commensurate with our aspirations for peace, love, and union with Source.

- We are an integral part of the evolutionary journey. In our genes are all generations of experience. In our genius is the code of conscious evolution. In our awakening lies the patterns of the planetary transition from our current phase to the next phase. Our mind is designed to know the design of evolution toward higher consciousness and freedom.

- This evolutionary process has a tendency toward higher consciousness and freedom through more complex or synergistic order, a tendency that is operative in us and can be accessed spiritually, socially, and scientifically. We are capable of resonating and cooperating with the tendency to fulfill our own greater potential and that of society as a whole.

- The universe is unitive, consistent throughout. There is one animating spiritual intelligence with infinitely diverse expressions of itself. Each of us is a living manifestation of that intelligence — sacred, unique, precious, and vital to the evolution of the whole.

Based on these assumptions, I believe we can say at this early stage of our new memetic code that conscious evolution provides us a natural value system as we observe the recurring patterns of evolution. We learn to value and work deliberately to cultivate greater consciousness and freedom through more complex and harmonious order. It gives us an internal relatedness to the cosmos and to all Earth life as members of one body. It provides us with an eschatology — a sense of end times, which for us is not the end of the world but rather the beginning of the new as we make our shift from self-conscious human to humans able to coevolve with nature and cocreate with Spirit.

It offers us a teleology, a sense of purpose and design in natural phenomena, that of becoming ever more cocreative with the universal tendency toward higher life. It offers a synthesis of *telos*, the study of ends, of final purposes, and *eros*, passionate love. In conscious evolution we become "telerotic" — in love with the fulfillment of the potential of the whole.

Conscious evolution provides an entelechy — a sense of ourselves when fully realized rather than merely potential. The possibility of becoming a cocreator, or universal human, which we have seen manifested in great beings such as Buddha and Jesus, can come to fruition in us. We recognize our growth motivation as the vital force of evolution urging us toward self-fulfillment and wholeness.

Conscious evolution gives us a context and logic for the emergence of the social potential movement. We are not working in a dying or meaningless universe. We are working in alignment with the whole process of creation. This process has a direction that is animating our heart's desire for greater freedom, union, and transcendence. The new meme encourages each of us to attune to our own creative urge, to express our potential for the sake of ourselves and the world. It urges us to find others and cocreate together. It gives meaning to the present as the fruition of evolution, the moment in which the wisdom of the entire past comes to life in the expression of each individual cocreator. Conscious evolution offers us the possibility of an open-ended, choiceful, glorious future. Within each of us stirs the mighty force of creation in the process of its next quantum transformation.

PART III

The Social Potential
Movement

CHAPTER NINE

From the Human Potential
to the Social Potential Movement

The social potential movement is the societal expression of conscious evolution. It has been latent throughout history because there has always been a longing in the human heart for a more just, free, loving, and creative society. But it was never before possible to fulfill these aspirations, because we had neither the evolutionary drivers and global crises to force us to change, nor did we have the scientific and technological powers that can free us from the limitations of scarcity, poverty, disease, and ignorance. This is the time of awakening for the social potential movement.

The social potential movement identifies peaks of social creativity and works toward social wellness and *social* actualization, just as the human potential movement identifies peak experiences in our personal lives and cultivates individual wellness and *self*-actualization. The movement seeks out innovations now working in health, environment, communication, education, government, economics, technology, and other fields of human endeavor while designing new social systems that lead toward a regenerative, life-enhancing global society.

Our aspirations for a society in which all people are free to be and do their best can now be fulfilled. We are speaking here of metamorphosis — the natural emergence of the societal butterfly.

Dee Ward Hock, the founder of Visa, wrote:

> We are at that very point in time when a 400-year-old age is dying and another is struggling to be born — a shifting of culture, science, society, and institutions enormously greater than the world has ever experienced. Ahead, the possibility of the regeneration of individuality, liberty, community, and ethics such as the world has never known, and a harmony with nature, with one another, and with the divine intelligence such as the world has never dreamed.[1]

The Path of the Cocreator

The foundation of the social potential movement is the emergence of the cocreative person, which has been the work of the human potential movement. We have been preparing for this path for thousands of years, through the great religious and ethical traditions, as previously mentioned. Yet only in our generation have we gained the actual powers of cocreation — the ability to become an integral part of the creative processes of nature and evolution.

In traditional religious language, we were created in the image of God and are becoming ever more godlike. In evolutionary language, we were created by the process of evolution and are becoming coevolutionary with that process. In cocreation we weave together two strands — our spiritual essence and our scientific and social capacities — to participate in the creation. When these strands blend, a new human is born: a universal human, one awakened through the heart to the whole of life, moved from within to express life purpose in the world, opening up to a cosmic consciousness. We become cocreators, unique and personal expressions of the divine, precisely because our creativity is so activated.

The most fundamental step on the path of the cocreator is a new spirituality in which we shift our relationship with the creative process from creature to cocreator — from unconscious to conscious evolution. Through resonance with the metapattern that connects us all, we learn to take responsibility for our part in the creation of our own evolution.

Building on the story of the Western world, the spiritual path of the cocreator — symbolically and mythologically — dawns on the *eighth* day of creation. In Genesis, God is said to have finished the work of the creation on the seventh day, rested, and saw that it was good. On the eighth day of creation, however, we are waking up to find that we are responsible for the creation. To fulfill this responsibility, we must gain an ever greater resonance with the process of creation, or in traditional terms, with the will of God. We are speaking here of nothing less than the spiritual maturation of humanity.

Out of this emerging cocreative spirituality comes the cocreative person. The cocreative person is one who is motivated by Spirit, awakened in the heart, and activated to express unique creativity for the sake of the self and the world. Although such persons have existed occasionally throughout history, never before has the genius within masses of us been called forth and expressed. The cocreative person is a new archetype on Earth. Its emergence is signaled by the shift from maximum procreation to cocreation. This archetype is emerging during the period of our birth, when Earth is reaching her population limits.

In my own life, the shift from procreation to cocreation changed everything. I found, as a mother of five, that after a certain point a deep yearning arose in my heart. Although I adored my children and husband, I became depressed. Through my study of Abraham Maslow's work, I could see that the depression was caused by the yearning to find and express unique vocation. "The feminine cocreator" is what I call the new feminine archetype of the woman who embodies and expresses the creative force within her to give birth to her authentic feminine self and its expression in the world. It is a second form of motherhood. The same is true of men. As they move beyond the hierarchical social structures of modern life, they too begin the search for authentic vocation and cooperation with others.

As people have fewer children and live longer lives with greater awareness, opportunity, and mobility, the cocreative person is appearing by the millions. We could describe ourselves as imaginal cells, cultural creatives proliferating and finding vocational partners in organic functions in the body of the social caterpillar just before metamorphosis.

The loving energy that went into self-reproduction is now available for self-evolution. This energy seeks to express life purpose. Just as we each have a genetic code, we also have a genius code — our individual creativity, the creator-within, now awakening and deeply desirous of expression in the world. Our spirituality is coming forth in spirit-motivated creative action.

The cocreative person is born when we experience an inner calling and say yes to that calling. In cocreation we are saying yes to the birth of our full potential self — that we will go the whole way in identifying our life purpose and bringing it forth as best we can into the world. This is as great a commitment as the birth and nurturance of a newborn child. As we become cocreative persons, our intimate relationships change. We are no longer primarily the procreative couple. Men and women join now, not only to have a child, but also to help give birth to each other, to support each other in full self-expression. As the old family structure breaks up, the new cocreative family emerges, based not only on the joining of our genes to have a child, but also on the joining of our genius to give rise to our full, creative selves.

The drive to cocreate is rising as the need for maximum procreation declines. Many of us are experiencing *vocational arousal*, the wild and exciting desire to find our calling. But society does not yet have the social or economic systems in place to nurture and support the expression of this untapped creativity. Establishing new systems that can call forth our best is the work of the social potential movement. A sea of creativity is welling up from within us, which is evolving our world. It is this creativity that new social innovations seek to further release and connect. Through new forms of education, new economic systems, social entrepreneurship, participatory management, and team-building and learning organizations, the social potential movement is learning how to channel this loving and creative energy for the social good.

The Convergence of Awareness and Action

Our personal growth has set the stage for the awakening of the social potential movement. It is relatively easy to evolve ourselves and our intimate relationships in family and at work. But what about the larger world? We look outside ourselves and we see social chaos, degradation, and overwhelming, complex problems — environmental degradation, overpopulation, resource depletion, hunger, poverty, social injustice, and alienation. To many, it seems impossible to solve these problems. We just do not have the time or the resources to coordinate a planetary economic and ecological system as rapidly as seems to be necessary to sustain and renew our threatened life-support systems. Some observers claim we have but a few decades to change our behavior in order to survive.

If we are really at this threshold of evolution or extinction, as Ervin Laszlo suggested, what could naturally facilitate this shift in time to save our world from the tragedies of environmental collapse or further social misery, hunger, poverty, and pain?

I believe there are two critical elements that can ease our transition and bring new hope for our fulfillment in the third millennium. One is the mass alignment of the consciousness that is already shifting toward a more unitive stage.

Creating events that align the consciousness of those already shifting toward a more cosmic, unitive form of awareness is vital. By reinforcing our higher consciousnesses through resonance with others, we are infusing what Rupert Sheldrake called the "morphogenetic field," as described earlier, and are making unitive consciousness more accessible to all people. These events are initiated whenever two or more kindred souls come together to reinforce each other's emergent qualities of being. We need vast celebrations that can catalyze a critical mass of people to experience a sense of oneness, empathy, and relatedness as members of one global family: a great awakening.

Another vital element in easing the transition is to find a way to accelerate connections among innovations currently working to change the world so that untapped creativity is channeled into meaningful work that expresses the individual's unique creativity. By connecting the dots of what's working, we'll also be allowing the vital functions in our one social body to communicate and work more effectively together.

An increased alignment of unitive consciousness combined with increased interaction among creative innovations is critical to a more gentle transition to the next stage of our evolution. The good news is that both elements are possible and, in fact, are beginning to happen. What we are suggesting here is a small nudge in the direction of greater convergence of the positive.

Nature's Secret Revealed

Is the convergence of our higher consciousness and expanded creativity enough to tip the scales in favor of a positive future, given the rapid escalation of problems that threaten our survival? I believe the answer is yes, because it is the nature of nature to repattern itself quickly when in conditions of extreme instability, such as we are experiencing through our environmental crisis. Although there are no certainties — we are potentialists, not optimists or pessimists — we can find a logical basis for pragmatic hope in the fabulous, unimaginable 13.8-billion-year journey of transformation. Our new story of creation has revealed to us five lessons of evolution. We have seen that:

- quantum transformations are nature's tradition;
- nature creates radical newness;
- crises precede transformation;
- problems are evolutionary drivers;
- holism is inherent in the nature of reality;
- nature takes jumps by creating new whole systems, greater than and different from the sum of their parts;
- evolution creates beauty, and everything that endures is beautiful;
- evolution raises consciousness and freedom through more complex order.

These recurring patterns give us a basis for hope. They express an evolutionary value system given to life itself as a pattern that has been generated for billions of years. It is now possible to align ourselves with these recurring patterns more consciously. Yet, to actually cooperate with nature, to align ourselves with the patterns of creation, we must know something more of how nature evolves. Our question must now be, How did nature rise from subatomic particles to you and me?

Does nature's capacity to take quantum jumps, to create more complex whole systems with ever greater capacity, give us any hints as to how we may consciously guide our evolution? I believed the answer was waiting for us, hidden in nature's 13.8 billion years of experience. Yet I searched for years to find the missing link that could help us get across the abyss from one quantum jump to the next.

I discovered a vital clue in the *New York Times* on October 12, 1977. That single article was tremendously helpful in my search to understand how we could make a quantum jump from our current social crises to an immeasurable future. The headline read "A Chemist Told How Life Could Defy Physics Laws."[2] The physicist was Nobel Prize winner Ilya Prigogine (pronounced *prig-a-gene*). He discovered the process whereby life evolves into more complex systems given the Second Law of Thermodynamics. This law states that in a closed system energy inevitably increases in entropy or disorder. Based on this "fatal" law, scientists have predicted that the universe will inevitably end in a "heat death" — the degradation of all matter and energy in the universe to an ultimate state of inert uniformity. In other words, all the stars in the billions of galaxies will burn out and destroy their planetary systems. Life as we know it is but a momentary use of this dying energy and will be destroyed with no hope for life to continue in a universe so structured that it inevitably dies. This law formed the scientific basis of much of modern pessimism.

The questions become: How, then, has life increased in "negentropy," or order, for billions of years? How, in the face of this inevitable tendency for the universe to increase in disorder, has more complex order increased for billions of years and is presumably still increasing? What are the mechanisms whereby higher order is achieved in nature? And, how might we learn from this process to facilitate our own leap to higher order — toward greater freedom, love, awareness, spirituality, and the proper use of tangible and intangible resources the universe has provided for us?

Prigogine found a clue in his theory of dissipative structures. A dissipative structure is an open system in nature whose form, or structure, is maintained by a continuous dissipation, or consumption of energy. All living systems are dissipative structures — including humans. In *The Aquarian Conspiracy*, Marilyn Ferguson described how "living things have been running uphill in a universe that is supposed to be running down."

Ferguson continued in her discussion of Prigogine:

> The continuous movement of energy through the system results in fluctuations; if they are minor, the system damps them and they do not alter its structural integrity. But if the fluctuations reach a critical size, they perturb the system. They increase the number of novel interactions within it.... The elements of the old pattern come into contact with each other in new ways and make new connections. The parts reorganize into a new whole. The system escapes into a higher order. As Prigogine said, at higher levels of complexity, the nature of the laws of nature changes. Life feeds on entropy. It has the potential to create new forms by allowing a shake-up of old forms. The elements of a dissipative structure cooperate to bring about this transformation of the whole.[3]

When I read this, I felt like a detective searching to understand how our own society could immediately make a quantum jump from our current crises to a future equal to our new powers. We cannot get there by linear, incremental steps alone, given the world's accumulating crises. But the process of transformation is not linear! Systems become more complex by nonlinear, exponentially increasing numbers of interactions of incremental innovations. At some point, apparently insignificant innovations connect in a nonlinear manner. Everything that rises converges and connects, becomes synergistic and cocreative. The system then cooperates in its own self-transcendence in an apparent sudden shift. This shift has been building for a long time out of myriad innovations silently and invisibly interacting and connecting beneath the surface of our attention — the work of early imaginal cells in the body of the disintegrating caterpillar.

Let's apply the Prigogine model to our personal and social evolution. If nature has been working through dissipative structures for billions of years, the same process must be working through us now. We can better facilitate the natural and ease all our transitions when we understand the process.

Human society is a large dissipative structure that is increasingly perturbed and is undergoing fluctuations. In our communities, systems are increasingly unstable or dysfunctional. We are using more of our energy to handle these problems in ways that seem ineffective, like building more weapons and prisons for greater security or fighting a war against drugs when kids roam aimlessly in the streets with nothing to do and nowhere to go. Hunger, poverty, social and economic injustice, violence in our communities and schools, resource depletion, pollution, overpopulation, the loss of rain forests, toxic wastes — all are escalating and all tend to converge in catastrophe.

Meanwhile, social innovations, or "improved mutations," are springing up everywhere. Thousands of acts of caring, sharing, healing, and new solutions are emerging. Applying the model of dissipative structures to our situation, we see that social innovations that share a similar value system are converging, connecting, and networking at an increasing rate. This process is accelerating rapidly through the internet. However, will the convergence of positive innovations happen before the convergence of destructive tendencies? Will the planetary system repattern to a higher order, or will it fall apart into chaos, into environmental collapse that has also been predicted? This is the question. There is no guarantee that a dissipative structure will repattern to a higher order. It is merely a tendency, just as it is the tendency of each baby to survive, although many do not.

It is precisely at this point that we need a new social innovation to facilitate the increased interaction among positive innovations — a new ground of the whole to facilitate this convergence.

This *is* the first age of conscious evolution. We must enter the process of our own evolution consciously. How can we do this? We can set in motion a new social function to hasten the nonlinear interaction of positive social innovations and to facilitate the natural repatterning of our society to a more harmonious order, thus saving ourselves from the predicted catastrophes.

CHAPTER TEN

Testing the Waters

After I discovered a clue, with the help of the Prigogine model, as to how nature evolves, I wanted to find a way to test my discovery in the real world. I had moved to Washington, DC, in 1970 and later cofounded the Committee for the Future, an organization whose purpose was to bring positive options for the future into the public arena for discussion and action. I was connected with innovators and potentialists throughout the country. As we were approaching 1984 — known as the Year of the Woman — at the urging of Buckminster Fuller I decided to do an experiment in conscious evolution by bringing the ideas of Abraham Maslow, Teilhard de Chardin, Fuller, and many other new paradigm thinkers into the political arena. I became an "idea candidate" for the future of humanity, offering a new social function to accelerate the interaction of positive innovations and help the system repattern itself without further violence, suffering, or environmental degradation.

I formed the Campaign for a Positive Future and told all my

friends and colleagues that I was in the running for selection as the Democratic vice-presidential candidate. (To be chosen by whomever was nominated for president as his vice-presidential candidate.) I asked them to arrange opportunities for me to speak in order to gain support for my ideas. Most of them were really surprised, yet delighted. Meetings were arranged, and I set out upon the most fascinating journey of my life.

A Campaign for What Works

To launch the campaign I created a new social function called the Office for the Future, or Peace Room (I used the two names interchangeably). The Peace Room was focused not only on Peace but also on the synergistic coordination of everything that is working toward a viable, sustainable, evolvable world. The reason I used the term "Peace Room" was because I wanted to compare its sophistication with what it takes to run a war room. This function would develop the idea of converging social innovations at the highest level of power. It was to reside in the office of the vice president of the United States (which, I believe, is still an underdeveloped office). Under the direction of the vice president, the Office for the Future was to become as sophisticated as a war room. In our war rooms we track enemies and strategize how to defeat them, so in our Peace Room we identify, map, connect, and communicate our successes, breakthroughs, and models that work. (Peace, in this context, is not defined as conflict resolution, as important as that is. It means peace through cocreation, through the full expression of human creativity in cooperation with nature, with one another, and with the deeper design of evolution.)

I proposed that the Office for the Future should have four functions that would facilitate the repatterning of our society to a higher order of consciousness, freedom, and synergy.

1. The office would scan for breakthroughs in all fields — health, education, media, science, government, business, the arts, community — wherever a person or small group invents or discovers something that creates a more life-enhancing world. Small acts to great projects would be noted. It would invite citizens at the local level to form centers to scan their communities for creative innovations; our ambassadors would be asked to establish Peace Rooms to discover what works in their countries. (I did not realize at the time that what was missing was internet technology.) I imagined that the world would be involved in discovering what is working and mapping, connecting, and communicating it around the globe. Can you imagine asking, "What's working in Iran, in Libya, in Sudan?" David L. Cooperrider said, "The more an organization [or any group or nation] experiments with the conscious evolution of positive imagery, the better it will become. There is an observable self-reinforcing, educative effect of affirmation. Affirmative competence is the key to the self-organizing system."[1]

2. The office would map these innovations according to function and geography to discover the pattern and design of what works. The anatomy of the social body would emerge. For example, in the area of education, all projects working on specific aspects of education, such as gifted children, lifelong learning, emotional maturity, and so forth, would be clustered in organic patterns until we could actually see the anatomy of what is working in each precise function of the social body. Soon we would have a picture of the emerging world. We envisioned large maps and graphs in the White House of progress toward the evolutionary agenda — the hierarchy of social needs

— with constant input based on what the people are doing that works.

As a part of the official United States Bicentennial Celebration in 1976, the Committee for the Future organized a synergistic convergence conference called SYN-CON in Washington, DC, with futurist Alvin Toffler, author of *Future Shock* and *The Third Wave*.[2] We graphically presented the hierarchy of social needs on a huge chart. People were calling in from all over the country with their social innovations, which were placed on the chart where they belonged as they contributed toward meeting an aspect of the evolutionary agenda (meeting basic, growth, and transcendent need levels). We saw how the whole social system was evolving in a coherent way. The apparent chaos of social change became coherent when the separate items were placed where they fit best in the hierarchy of social needs. We saw the social body as a living system in transition from one stage of its evolution to the next, evolving through the myriad acts that countless unrelated individuals were doing. I used the metaphor of the Rose Window at Chartres Cathedral. Each pane of stained glass alone seems meaningless and insignificant, but when it becomes a part of the whole pattern of the Rose Window it is magnificent. Just so, each act alone may seem unimportant or random, but when allowed to self-organize as part of a living system, each act finds its natural place within the social body and is thereby seen to be a vital and even sacred part of the whole. Through this process we see the design of evolution, and each person can better find their unique place within the evolving system. The plan of action unfolds based on what is already working.

3. The office would connect people and projects for greater cooperation and effectiveness. It would be a powerful, upgraded networking function to help social innovators make vital connections needed with others. The deep human desire to relate, to connect, to join our genius is satisfied when we find our teammates and partners. Cocreation does not mean service at the sacrifice of self; it means service through the actualization of self. Self-actualization occurs when we find our vocations and express them meaningfully in the world. Our vocations are drawn forth by the process of finding others we need, by enlivening our individual lives and the quality of life in the community.

4. The office would communicate via all media the stories of the human family's successes and model projects. I suggested there be a weekly broadcast from the White House — "What Works in America" — calling for greater public participation, inviting people to join projects, to start new projects, to find their life purpose and come together to create the works and acts needed for the future of the human family. Volunteerism would come alive as the expression of our love and creativity in chosen work.

I sent out a "high-fidelity bird call," as economist Hazel Henderson put it, and I got a certain kind of bird, all imaginal cells ready to join to cocreate a new and better world. Many had not been active in politics because, like myself, they had not thought they could make much of a difference. It was thrilling. Everywhere I went people said they wanted to form a center for it — whatever *it* is. *It* was not quite a political philosophy or a new party; *it* wasn't political at all, in the old sense of the word.

Although no one thought I would actually be vice president, I stated my goal to make a speech at the Democratic National

Convention on global media, declaring that the purpose of the
United States of America is to liberate the creativity of people
everywhere. I promised that, as vice president, I would build an
Office for the Future and a Peace Room in the White House and
ask all ambassadors in every country to do the same. Within four
years, I said, we would find out what is working in the world.

During my campaign, I discovered that the *it* that people
longed for was the center, the creative essence in each person
awakened, amplified, connected, and manifested in creative action
to serve some need in ourselves as well as in the community. People sought communion, community, and cocreativity, not something that any leader could do for them. It was what we could do
for others by coming together in a new way. Yet, people found it
exciting to have a political candidate support them in their initiatives and raise their aspirations to a national level. What was also
very important was that we had a specific goal with a time frame:
by July 24, we would need two hundred delegates to sign their
names for me to be nominated for vice president.

As I went around the country speaking, little centers sprung
up everywhere, calling themselves Positive Future Centers. They
were actually embryonic centers for cocreation. The people med-
itated and prayed; they worked on themselves and they reached
into their communities, making their contributions to express
their life purpose. Wherever I went I was at home. Even as a wife
and mother raising my children, I'd had a strange longing for a
deeper belonging. Now I had found it. Those little centers felt like
home, a place for us to flock together, try our wings, and learn to
fly. Each center was resonant with the evolutionary agenda and
affirmed the new paradigm. People were interested in both the
human and the social potential. They were eager to carry the
inner work into the world. People sought to bring their love and
creativity into the community, learning to repattern the larger

world in the image of their higher selves. Ninety Positive Future Centers formed. My campaign manager, Carolyn Anderson, and I discovered a recurring pattern in each of the centers. They had begun to form heart-centered circles that cultivated resonance and sharing toward social innovation and creativity. In her book (cowritten with Katharine Roske) *The Co-Creator's Handbook*, she discussed these *evolutionary circles*, which we later called *cocreative cores*.[3]

Our goal was to model the change we wanted to see in the world. Only if we ourselves could evolve, could our society transform. "The best solution is our own conscious evolution," was one of our slogans. We began the work of politics from the inside out, on the personal level, while realizing that we needed systemic changes on the social scale.

I asked for leaders at the growing edge of every field to meet and discuss the options for a positive future. Buckminster Fuller was my mentor, along with Willis Harman, former president of the Institute of Noetic Sciences (founded by astronaut Edgar Mitchell to research the science of consciousness), family therapist Virginia Satir, and other outstanding innovators and creators of the new paradigm.

However, when the time came to attend the Democratic National Convention, politically sophisticated people told me, "Don't go to San Francisco, dear. You have done a good job at the grassroots level, but they will destroy you at a national convention." We had no money left, no media attention (we were told we were too positive), and no passes to the floor (the Democratic National Committee had ignored our campaign, telling us that the kind of person we were attracting was too self-centered to be of any value to them politically). Liberal political leaders felt that human potentialists were narcissistic and not to be taken into account, for in fact, we had not been active before. Traditional

Democrats focused on helping those oppressed and victimized, rather than empowering each other to free ourselves. Obviously both are needed, but we were the newer element, and had not yet found our voice. (Now there are more than eighty million cultural creatives, many of whom are transformationally motivated, in the United States alone.[4] A mighty force has arisen in the intervening years.)

However impossible it seemed from any rational logic, ten of us decided to go to the convention, for my guidance was that we had not yet completed the mission of having my name placed in nomination for the vice presidency. My purpose was to speak at the convention and call for the Office for the Future and the Peace Room, which would tell the story of humanity's evolutionary potential in a political context and plant the idea of the evolutionary agenda and a transformed presidency focused on what works.

Our task was to have two hundred delegates sign a petition that would place my name in nomination so I could make my nominating speech before the convention, the nation, and the world. Doubt raged, for I had enough sense as a political science graduate to know that this was impossible. I should give up before suffering the humiliation of being totally ignored, for the chances of a grassroots, futuristic, unknown woman being nominated for the vice presidency of the United States were less than zero. I was told we would be lucky to get one delegate, even if she were my mother!

We decided, however, to act as if we were going to succeed and to practice every metaphysical discipline any of us had learned. We arose at five every morning. We prayed; we loved one another; we forgave one another; we did creative visualizations of the nominating speech; we affirmed our victory with certainty; and, most important, we overcame doubt, using the technology of creating the future through structural tension.

Our team continually chose and rechose our goal (no matter how impossible it seemed) while making friends with current reality — not denying anything about the truth of our situation. The tension between the goal and the current condition can snap one, like a taut rubber band released, toward the goal. And it did.

We went into the hallways, the bars, the restaurants, and the early-morning caucuses to sign up delegates. Occasionally I was given thirty seconds to speak at the caucuses. I was able to say, "My name is Barbara Marx Hubbard. I am running for the vice presidency to propose an Office for the Future that will scan for, map, connect, and communicate positive innovations that work." Although there were many famous political activists trying for this nomination, the delegates decided to give me the chance to speak for them to the world. They signed up! And I wasn't the only one who obtained the signatures. The ten people who formed the team — only one had been to a national convention — obtained most of the signatures. The resonance we had created among ourselves radiated and seemed to mesmerize the busy delegates. They really had no intention of nominating me for vice president, but there was an *X factor*, a special appeal that attracted them to sign, almost against their better judgment.

The first day we had one hundred signatures. The second day we had another hundred. On the third day, my campaign manager, Faye Beuby, took the petitions to the Democratic National Committee at the convention. We had more than two hundred signatures. The Committee was horrified! Someone had gotten through the net. But to their credit they verified the petitions and authorized my nomination, although they moved up the convention two hours so that my speech would not get national prime time, only C-SPAN. Then the announcement came: two women's names were to be placed in nomination for the vice presidency of the United States: Barbara Marx Hubbard and Geraldine Ferraro.

I was stunned. It was a political paranormal experience! The impossible had happened.

I rushed to write the speech, "To Fulfill the Dream," that we had been visualizing in so many church basements, living rooms, and small groups. When I was taken to the huge dais to speak, a guard led me to the microphone, holding my arm gently. "Honey," he said, "don't worry, they won't pay any attention to you, they never do...you're saying this for the universe." And so I did. I said, "The purpose of the United States of America is to emancipate the creativity of people everywhere." I adapted a passage from the Declaration of Independence, saying:

> We hold these truths to be self-evident:
> All people are born creative,
> endowed by our Creator
> with the inalienable right and responsibility
> to express our creativity
> for the sake of ourselves and our world.

I proposed a choiceful future, a time when we would join together to meet basic needs, to restore the environment, to educate ourselves to realize our full potential, and to explore the further reaches of the human spirit and our expanded environment in space. With all the power of my being I called for the new social function, the Peace Room, in the White House. The delegates were milling around, paying no attention, but as I spoke the words, I realized for the first time the enormous power of focused action and faith. If a disorganized band of grassroots environmentalists, businesspeople, housewives, futurists, and human potentialists could achieve this, imagine what we could do if we were well organized. The speech, "Barbara Marx Hubbard — 1984 Democratic National Convention speech," can be seen on YouTube.

The Next Step

I learned from the campaign that the appeal of the new social function — to connect the positive — is almost irresistible. It was literally a political paranormal experience to have my name placed in nomination. It happened because the idea is obvious and intuitively almost all people want it to happen.

Secondly, I realized that in this campaign there were seeds of a new approach to politics that could work. Mine was a symbolic idea campaign; I am not a politician. I do not have organizing skills. I am a communicator of ideas and a stimulator of vision. From the campaign's modest, yet remarkable, success, however, I saw how a real team might succeed in transforming American politics, opening it up to a more participatory and creative democracy.

A presidential and vice-presidential team should form and select ahead of time members of a cabinet who know well the social innovations in their fields. The team would work together, discover, and link up with what is now working to create a positive future. After they have identified key innovations in each field, they would spend the needed time developing a platform based on the further development of what works. It is a design for a positive future. The presidential candidate would introduce the team the American people will actually be electing if they elect the candidate president. Each team member would speak briefly about what he or she knows really works for solving a problem. The team would then introduce major social innovators who briefly discuss the success of their projects. The vice-presidential candidate would promise to establish the Office for the Future in the White House.

The presidential team would invite people to tell them more of what works in each region of the country and ask them to form local centers to continue to scan for, map, connect, and communicate breakthroughs in their communities. These campaign events would attract local media and elected officials. Efforts would be made to connect people and projects and to continually facilitate cocreation among people. The presidential team would become a magnet for the positive. Using the internet, the team could not only connect and communicate the positive in this country, but could join with teams in other countries who choose to do the same for their societies. We would quickly cultivate a new movement for positive change rising throughout the world.

I believe that such a campaign would have a beneficent effect on the political process and would inspire candidates from all parties and at all levels of government to run on the people's innovation and creativity.

My sense is that the timing is right to take the next step in the manifestation of this vision. The Cold War, in its most deadly form, is over. The insane threat of nuclear winter has receded. Yet the crises afflicting our system, especially the environment, are escalating. Paradoxically, at the same time, the materialistic or pessimistic worldview is transforming as the number of cultural cocreatives rises. However, there is currently no comprehensive hopeful meme to guide our actions toward a positive future. I propose that conscious evolution offers such a vital worldview and a set of memes and social processes that can guide us through this evolutionary shift.

The desire for liberal democracy is rising throughout the world, yet liberal democracy as we have known it is failing everywhere. There are evolutionary reasons for this fact. It's structured wrongly. It's oppositional. It's win-lose. It's controlled by money. It's dissociated from the grass roots and seeks power to stay in office. It does not cultivate cooperation but forces a win-lose competition. And to get media attention, people and parties exaggerate their differences.

More recently in the Arab Spring, the Occupy Wall Street movement, and elsewhere throughout the world, the people have risen up. But so far there has not been a political process equal to the way nature actually takes jumps during times of crises. To actually create the next stage of democracy, we need to pioneer forms of "social synergy," the political expression of nature's capacity to take jumps by radical exponential interaction of innovating elements. This has to be done now.

The desire for better systems of governance is rising throughout the world. People are demanding the right to choose, both socially and personally. And people are increasingly aware of what is *not* working. Growing numbers are outraged by economic and social injustice affecting millions in the United States and billions throughout the world. Yet, solutions are also becoming better known through the expanding networking of organizations and groups, the astonishing growth of the internet, and the growing interest in positive news.

As I have mentioned, the planet has grown a new nervous system. The internet has allowed for a level of connectivity we have never seen before. We now need a "synergy engine," or a process of cocreation and collaboration, to help us use the internet even more effectively. It could foster the largest mass uprising of creativity the world has ever known, and we are right at the threshold.

Globalization is accelerating and is having a major impact on our noosphere. It is empowering us to address en masse the seminal questions of the direction and values of society in the twenty-first century. In this world where old familiar memes are failing to guide us toward a positive future, the new meme of conscious evolution is already beginning to serve people seeking deeper direction and meaning in their lives.

In the past decades, the human potential movement has

matured. People are learning a deep level of personal responsibility for their lives and are ready to reach into their communities. Cultural creatives have emerged as the fastest growing subculture in the world. They are gaining influence in all fields of endeavor.

Furthermore, technological breakthroughs foster this movement, especially the internet. Are we heading for new forms of sustainable growth or toward environmental or economic collapse? No one knows. It depends on what we do personally and collectively. But I sense that there is enough positive movement to feel hopeful. It reminds me of the moment just after the birth of an infant, just before its nervous system has linked up, while it is still womb oriented and panicked...yet beginning to breathe and opening its still-dimmed eyes.

Since my campaign people have continually asked, "When is the Peace Room going to come into being?" Now is the time to fully engage that question in service of our conscious evolution.

CHAPTER ELEVEN

A Spirit-Motivated Process of Action for the Twenty-First Century

---

From the perspective of the social potential movement, our goal for the twenty-first century should be a broad acceptance of the evolutionary agenda, supported by the worldview of conscious evolution and manifested through new social innovations and social systems that lead toward a positive and ever-evolving future as a universal humanity, an emerging humanity. My vice-presidential campaign was an early initiative to bring this idea into the public arena. The key to its success (at that time before the internet was readily available) was the pragmatic proposal to build the Peace Room to scan for, map, connect, and communicate what is working in the world. This was a metasocial innovation that could reinforce all innovations and facilitate the social dissipative structure to repattern itself to a higher order of complexity, consciousness, freedom, and capacity.

The Peace Room formed the basis of what organizational development specialist David Cooperrider called an appreciative inquiry: "a process to seek out the best of 'what is' to help ignite the collective imagination of 'what might be.' Its aim is to generate knowledge that expands the realm of the possible, helping us envision a collectively desired future and carry forth that vision in ways that successfully translate images of possibility into reality."[1]

More recently, Otto Scharmer introduced the concept of "presencing" — learning from the emerging future — in his bestselling books *Theory U* and *Presence: An Exploration of Profound Change in People, Organizations, and Society*, which he coauthored with Peter M. Senge, Joseph Jaworski, and Betsy Sue Flowers.[2]

We might say poetically that we are aiming at a social lunar landing. In the 1960s John F. Kennedy proclaimed that "we would land a man on the moon and bring him back alive within the decade." When I first wrote this book in the 1990s, the idea of building a Peace Room was for the social potential movement the equivalent of what a lunar landing was to technologists in the 1960s. But now that the internet has created a space for people to connect in the ways I envisioned a Peace Room would allow people to do, we must update our vision.

What goal could we choose that, if achieved, would be a definitive change, a milestone for the social potential movement like the lunar landing was for the technologists? I believe this goal should be to create and implement a set of events across the planet in which a critical mass of people worldwide will connect with one another via the internet and in person to cocreate and activate what's working in the world. This is a "global moon shot."

This initiative will catalyze a movement toward a conscious civilization and an effort toward sustainability and cooperation with one another and the environment — and ultimately the next stage of evolution itself. It will lead toward an expanded, democratic, and inclusive effort to facilitate the transition from one phase of evolution to the next. In every region of the world people would scan for, map, connect, and communicate what is working toward a humane, regenerative world — a cocreative society and an ever-evolving future, both on Earth and in the solar system and beyond. Each nation and culture would strive to find its own way to empower its transformational leadership at the frontiers of positive change. In the United States, for example, we might have a transformed American presidency that reflects and is supported by the values and structures of the social potential movement. But this will not happen unless we the people take the lead.

To achieve these goals we need a plan or, more accurately, a process of action. As mentioned, the higher up one goes in the existing social structures, the harder it is to make the change. The real changes will come from accelerating the interaction of what is already working among people in every field and function.

This does not mean that suddenly everyone will become positive, peaceful, and loving toward one another. It just means that at times of critical instability in the existing system, small islands of coherence in a sea of social chaos can jump the system to a higher order of consciousness, freedom, and connectivity. We are advocating here that those who are *already* predisposed to positive action and resonance with one another join together in time to avoid the devastating collapse of our life-support system now being foreseen.

Ervin Laszlo said informally to a group of us at a large global cultural forum in China in 2014: "Either we will join together for an ecological civilization in the next five years, or we will be extinct!" The question is, "What can we do to make this change quickly enough, before it's too late?"

This "spirit-motivated process of action" is a pragmatic suggestion that the best approach we can take is for people and projects already evolving toward a peaceful, sustainable, and evolvable world to join together in social synergistic initiatives.

We need to "network the networks" of positive change, people already participating in restoring the Earth, freeing ourselves from hunger, poverty, and war, and exploring the vast reaches of Spirit within and the universe beyond.

This process requires grassroots leadership. The Foundation for Conscious Evolution will play its part, but the process cannot be led by any one group alone. Only cooperation and synergy among leaders of positive change will be capable of generating the wisdom, know-how, and processes to shift the system to a higher order.

When a critical mass of people worldwide participates in such a nonlinear, exponential interaction of innovations and solutions, the system can cooperate in its own self-transcendence. This is what is suggested in Ilya Prigogine's understanding of dissipative structures: how nature has evolved from increasing disorder (entropy) to more complex order (syntropy), as from single-celled to multicelled organisms, to humans with 50 trillion cells each, and now to planet Earth itself being linked into one interacting, intercommunicating organism through our global nervous system.

This process of networking the networks could awaken what Teilhard de Chardin called "the noosphere," the consciousness of the peoples of Earth, to turn on its "collective eyes" in the field of global heart coherence. Teilhard imagined that this level of connectivity would catalyze a communion of love worldwide.

We would find that we do have the resources, technologies, and know-how to make the world work for all, as predicted by Buckminster Fuller. This would release countless people from fear of lack and destruction. It would stimulate what Abraham Maslow called the self-actualizing person to discover and act upon "self-rewarding work," their core functions or life purposes in chosen work. It would help people find partners to cocreate with, awakening the greater genius in people everywhere. It would catalyze the "self-actualizing society," by awakening the power of our social potential as called for in this book.

Rather than trying to persuade those who want to uphold the status quo, we need to invite those already moving toward positive change. (This movement is motivated by attraction — *evolution by attraction*.) Doing so will engender a massive uprising of creativity and *vocational arousal*. Vocational arousal occurs in each of us when our life purpose is excited and turns on. We seek teammates and partners to join not our genes to create babies but rather our genius to give birth to our greater selves and our world, as I have said before.

The same capacities that have empowered humanity to survive and grow to billions of people inhabiting Earth are now manifesting in many of us as the yearning to express greater potential, to join to cocreate and participate in meaningful action and heartfelt community. This will result in a coming together of people everywhere who are in jobs and positions that are less than who they truly are. It will be a mass movement of the heart and the head together. To achieve these goals we need new structures to hold a collaborative process among pioneers in social innovation and media.

During an Apollo mission, Dr. Thomas Paine, the NASA administrator at the time, showed me the flowchart that guided the hundreds of thousands of separate tasks required for the lunar landing. At the very end of the huge flowchart was a big picture of an astronaut. Under it were the words "bring him back alive." I imagined a planetary flowchart and a global Peace Room process that would offer a self-mapping, self-tracking schema of emerging creative work, a sort of Wikipedia for myriad initiatives in every field of endeavor, an indicative plan made up of everyone's plans so that we could all see what one another was doing, correct our own activities, and be more effective through collaboration. The flowchart would culminate in a new goal: "bring us forward alive!"

The emergence of the internet has effectively made this vision possible. Through the internet, now almost any of us can map and track the types of social innovations that we are interested in and collaborate with each other in ways that would have been virtually unimaginable for most of the history of the human species.

Because the internet has done so much to create this potential flowchart and allow for collaboration around today's most brilliant social innovations, the next step is to cocreate a virtual process online through which we can capitalize on everything that technology and our new social innovations have to offer. It would be on the scale of Facebook or Twitter but with the purpose of creating a virtual space and community with a shared global intention of collective awakening through interconnectivity, resonance, and love. This virtual space could magnetize people to bring forth their next level of potential and allow them to find each other and connect in person to cocreate the next stage of our evolution. Connecting in person is just as vital as connecting virtually. Many of us are now sensing the need for this increase in interconnectivity among people and projects focused on what is working. The question is not if but *when* this will happen.

Noomap (www.noomap.info) is an exciting new initiative currently in development that might meet this need. According to the company's website, it aims to offer "an entirely novel, 'global brain' approach to the Internet. Noomap's mission is to evolve the planet into a living embodiment of the Noosphere... designed to connect individuals and communities by mapping the various aspects of our human creativity." It will be interesting to see how Noomap unfolds.

The Need for Collaboration

In the summer of 2013, I became aware of a Wisdom 2.0 talk by Justin Rosenstein, cofounder of Asana and inventor of Facebook's "Like" button. In his talk, he lays out his vision for how we can move from a me-focused society to a we-focused society by accelerating two key ideas — interconnectedness and universal love. Rosenstein referenced me in the talk as a futurist in conscious evolution, and he later followed up with me, asking how he could help us spark the new planetary birth experience.[3]

I would like to share one part of his vision here because it captures why and how collaboration can work in the coming decades. He wrote me in an email:

> I believe we can repurpose all our institutions — technology, business, governance, media, health, justice. These are ultimately human institutions (all created relatively recently), and together we can reprogram them in a way consistent with universal human values. Working together, a critical mass of inspired change-agents can manually transform each system. The first step is for all of us to align around a shared mission: *to help humanity thrive.* The second step is to get our hands dirty: to develop expertise in our respective fields and take practical steps to redesign our systems from the inside out, whether as leaders or individual contributors. We can rewrite the norms, stories, and behaviors of each of our institutions. It's a journey of a thousand miles, but organizations committed to our shared project are already taking big steps toward a more thriving world.

Rosenstein went on to say that the growing number of organizations working to apply technology toward human thriving heartens him. He cited the following innovative businesses as promising examples:

- Sungevity and SolarCity for using innovations in finance and satellite photography to provide zero-money-down solar paneling.
- Coursera, which helps anyone in the world with an internet connection get a first-class education.
- Lyft, which is devoted to decimating the number of cars a city needs by facilitating ridesharing.

He finished his email with this:

> To achieve humanity's potential, love must be *applied* in a deeply pragmatic way to make substantive, measurable impact on real-world systems. My proposal is that we come together to do that, as a team. As *one project*, unified not by a central leader or shared office building, but by a shared decision to participate, to contribute our unique gifts to the cause. Not by doing philanthropy on the side, but by devoting the bulk of our effort — our careers — to work that both satisfies our individual creative passions *and* has the potential for significant positive impact on the world. Together, that team will transform our world, one step at a time, into one of abundance, harmony, sustainability, wisdom, and boundless creative human expression.[4]

Rosenstein has captured the essence of the vital role that collaboration must play in the next stage of our conscious evolution. And many of us sense that this task is not something we can do on the side, but rather something we want to embody in all the dimensions of our life.

For Bharat Mitra, founder of Organic India and the Uplift Festival, his day job really did become a vehicle for activating his and other people's passions as well as their shared interest in significant positive upliftment. He wrote to me by email:

> Organic India was founded with the vision and inspiration to be a Vehicle of Consciousness — a living embodiment of love and consciousness in action beyond the delusion of separation between spirituality and the material world. We were called to bring into the corporate world a new model for business, grounded in the principles of nature, interconnectedness and the fundamental truth of oneness. Over the past 15 years, Organic India has become a global success story on the material plane, without ever compromising our core values and purpose.
>
> It is from this wellspring of vast possibility that UPLIFT was born as a festival of transformation in Byron Bay, Australia, in December 2012 to infuse the collective field with love and peace. The four-day festival and global webcast has become a thriving birthplace of new projects, inspired initiatives and global collaboration in service of humanity and Mother Earth. From this spirit and vision, unprecedented partnerships and possibilities have emerged in a very short amount of time, manifesting in projects in all areas of life including cleaning the Ganga, the rivers in India and waters of the world, empowering visionary youth activists and creating a collaborative global youth movement, mentoring conscious business leaders. Through this cocreative platform we have the capacity to reach millions of people around the world — infusing the human field with a shared experience of love and consciousness, and planting seeds of new initiatives that we all can join and be part of. Each one of us has our own unique gifts, purpose and role to play in this magnificent existence. It is only when we all come

together that this new era can manifest. We truly can create oneness in action in the world.[5]

These are a couple of examples of the kinds of groups and people that are initiating collaboration in awakening our collective potential. And while collaboration is integral to the conscious evolution movement, many other elements are also critical in activating the power of our social potential.

A New Social Architecture

Another vital step to sparking our social evolution and humanity's next level of awakening is to develop a new model of society as a whole system in transition. When we view society now, we see it in its confused and apparently incoherent state. Social innovations are dispersed throughout the social body, often ignored, disconnected, and underfunded.

Now let's develop our "evolutionary eye," a lens that sees from the evolutionary perspective. From this perspective, we can see our society as a living organism in transition.

Let's imagine our social body as a wheel divided into sectors that represent vital functions — health, education, environment, governance, and so on (we'll look at this wheel model in detail later in this chapter). Every system in the social body is currently under stress: environmental degradation, violence within communities, failing educational systems, and on and on. Yet it is equally true that there are breakthroughs in every field and function. We do not consistently notice the breakthroughs, for we lack the evolutionary lens. When we view the current situation with our evolutionary eye, we see the implicit pattern of success in every functional area.

When we identify and connect breakthroughs and solutions, we see the outlines of the emerging world. Each breakthrough or solution is a point of transformation created by innovators who are making something new work now. By connecting and communicating these innovations, we see elements of the design for a positive future in every field — not in the distant future, but as a pragmatic reality upon the frontiers of progress.

What We Mean by "What Works"

Along with the development of a model of the social body as a system in transition, we must deepen our inquiry into what we mean when we say that something "works." This question is vital — for the way we respond to it will guide our selection of social innovations. Values form the fundamental basis of ethical evolution, which must be quickly learned if we are to use our new powers for life-oriented purposes. The question "What do we mean by 'what works'?" leads us to the very nature of the new society we choose to cocreate. Obviously, we don't mean a better gun or a faster car. Values must be considered by all of us throughout society. There can be no dogma here, only openness and tolerance of differences. As we seek the underlying metapattern that connects, the implicate order becomes explicate.

As a student of evolution, I suggest there are values inherent in the whole process of creation that can serve as guidelines to us now. These values — the fifth lesson of evolution — are higher consciousness and greater freedom through more complex or synergistic order. Evolution has moved in this direction with every quantum jump. By consciously working toward these values now, we are cooperating with the process of creation, in alignment with a 13.8-billion-year trend!

From the evolutionary perspective, we value any act, intention, or belief that expands our consciousness toward a more unitive, spiritual, loving, whole-centered stage. We favor acts that support the ethics of all our religions to love one another, to "do unto others as we would have done unto ourselves," and to have reverence for higher dimensions of our own nature, for other species, and for Earth and the cosmos. Equally, we value acts that lead to greater freedom — freedom not only from deficiencies of hunger, poverty, and lack of self-esteem but also to realize our untapped potential for self-actualization and chosen life purpose. Freedom without higher consciousness and the compassionate responsibility for others as well as ourselves can become self-centered and destructive. Yet higher consciousness without freedom to act can become so inner directed that it cuts us off from social involvement, which is vital to the survival of humanity. This is the core reason why the social potential movement is so necessary now.

Finally, we select acts for the value of synergistic (win-win) order. This means we value whatever helps bring separate parts together into greater wholeness and cooperation — personally, in our intimate relationships, in our communities, and among religions, nations, disciplines, races, and cultures. We value what joins us together to form a whole society that is different from, unpredictable from, and greater than the sum of its parts — the definition of synergy. The quest for shared values is intrinsic to the social potential movement.

The Wheel of Cocreation

The social body can be modeled in a variety of ways. An excellent wheel design was developed in the 1970s by Avon Mattison, president of Pathways to Peace, and has been continually refined by many colleagues over the subsequent decades. It depicts the evolutionary process of peace — the dynamic in which we create the future in harmony with one another, with nature, and with Spirit. Although elsewhere it is named a Peace Wheel©, in this context we call it the Wheel of Cocreation. We have found that this Wheel is one of the best ways to bring the Peace Room's ideals to life.

The Wheel comprises twelve sectors, each of which is a vital system of the whole, offering a visible matrix of the emerging social body in which we place our creative acts. The functional pattern is composed of countless separate innovations. It is envisioned as a vast internet repository of organizations and initiatives divided into these twelve sectors, and people working toward conscious evolution will place their innovations in the sectors where they fit best. The Wheel is the context for the mother meme described in a previous chapter, calling to her heart all precious memelets — ideas that hold the seed of the emerging civilization.

The following are the Wheel's twelve sectors — the pathways to social transformation toward a peaceful, cocreative world — and the guidelines and goals of each one, suggesting some of the broad kinds of results we seek in each area.

THE SECTORS OF THE WHEEL OF COCREATION

1. Infrastructure

A vast rebuilding of the failing infrastructure can offer employment and meaningful work to millions. Renewable energy such as solar, wind, and thermal energy provides unlimited sources of power to meet growing needs.

2. Justice

Victim-offender reconciliation rehabilitates criminals rather than punishing them. The Restorative Justice movement brings together victims and offenders of a crime for dialogue and reconciliation and reduces the number of repeat offenses.

3. Media

Open-source social media encourages free, engaging, and empowering activism to address issues like poverty, violence, pollution, and so on. The "NewNews" model, proposed in chapter 13, requires an evolution of our concept of news itself to reporting on examples of what is emerging, creative, and actually new. It calls for us to become newsmakers ourselves. Through the internet and smartphones we are all potentially communicators of the new stories.

4. Relations

Cocreative relationships exemplify the shift from the domination to the partnership model, from the top-down structures of modern society to a new social architecture. We cultivate synergy and connectivity in all our relationships, from personal to social to planetary. The human potential, transpersonal, integral, psychosynthesis, and positive psychology movements are working toward the maturation of humanity from the kindergarten to the grown-up stage of behavior. The emergence of a deepening spirituality is releasing millions from devotion to an autocratic male God figure toward the embodiment and incarnation of the divine within.

5. Science

The great success of reductionist science in its early phases is shifting to include an expanded view of reality itself, suggesting a living universe, or multiverse, in which consciousness is primary. An underlying coherence and "entanglement" exists throughout the entire multiverse, and a vast field of knowledge, known as the Akashic field, is inherent there. Contact with extraterrestrial and extradimensional beings is investigated scientifically and through personal experiences.

6. *Spirituality*

Spirituality is deepening and diversifying as humanity is maturing. We sense an ever-deepening personal contact with the divine, the embodiment of Spirit, the incarnation of the impulse of evolution. "God" incarnates in us as we become conscious cocreators, merging with the creative process of the universe as a whole. An evolutionary spirituality is arising as we tap into our own higher guidance and our soul's purpose. The common values decreed by the great religions, such as "love your neighbor as yourself," are universalized as the next step of human behavior beyond any dogma.

7. *Arts*

Out of the early phases of modern art, which depicted the end of an era and the breakup of our past images of ourselves, new forms of art are arising: multimedia, sound and light, immersive media — simulations that touch the psyche of humanity with new myths, new visions, and new worlds.

8. *Economics*

A new economic paradigm is arising out of the breakdown of the top-down economic model that accrues vast wealth to 1 percent of humanity while billions of people struggle to live. Socially responsible investing is highly profitable. We are growing beyond the current monetary structure. New forms of complementary currencies are emerging. Sharing, caring, gift economies, and self-sufficient community living are arising as people join together to survive and thrive rather than competing to win.

9. *Education*

We are at the dawn of a new evolutionary educational system. Instead of breaking subjects into separate, unrelated disciplines, evolutionary education takes the holistic overview perspective, sees the process of creation as an unfolding pattern from the origin of creation to the present, and then places each of us in the story as its cocreators as we seek out our vocations, our places within the Wheel of Cocreation. We are learning from what works to evolve ourselves and our world during this period of ultimate crises and amid the requirement that we must change in order to survive. New modes of learning are expanding, including internet-based worldwide classes of all kinds, such as those on The Shift Network (www.theshiftnetwork.com) and Evolving Wisdom (www .evolvingwisdom.com).

10. *Environment*

Many of us begin to recognize that we are nature itself, all of us. The environment is within us, and we are within it. We are learning to preserve, restore, and cultivate our biosphere — our whole life-support system and all the endangered species — as part of our own survival. The greatest mass movement in history, as described by Paul Hawken in *Blessed Unrest*, is awakening millions who are responding to environmental and social problems of all kinds. Indigenous peoples and modern society are seeking to join forces to cultivate a sustainable, evolvable world. We realize that we ourselves are among the "endangered species" and that we must learn to coevolve with nature as we begin to cocreate with Spirit within us.

11. *Governance*

As current forms of governance are failing — from top-down dictatorships to liberal democracy based on win-lose voting and corporate control — civil society is arising as the real center of power. New forms of self-governance and management and new synergistic processes of organization are spreading. Security no

longer is assured by vast military forces, as small groups desta-
bilize the world out of anger and the illusion of separation. Networking the networks of positive change as described in this book
is a way to awaken the power of our social potential. We are on
the threshold of implementing a synergistic democracy, wherein
we seek common goals and match needs with resources.

12. Health

We are becoming aware that our body-minds are a whole system influenced by our thoughts, intentions, states of being, diet,
and self-care. We find we are capable of self-healing, and at the
same time we are making great strides in our medical technology,
improving longevity. With nanotechnology and genetics we may
become self-evolving beings. Eventually, as we choose to live
beyond the planets in the solar system, we face the possibility of
developing a new species, a cosmic species born out of our own
yearning to evolve. When the sun expands and destroys all planets in the solar system billions of years hence, we may be a galactic
species.

Golden Innovations

A vital function of the Wheel of Cocreation is to help identify
what social analyst and activist Eleanor LeCain called *golden innovations*. A golden innovation is a project now working successfully
that, if further developed and applied, could transform the system
in which it functions. It differs from a simply good innovation in
that it could have a quantum effect in addressing a major social ill.
Golden innovations are mutually reinforcing and interconnect-
ing. They foster intrinsic values by embodying greater cooperation, creativity, optimism, a tolerance for differences, a sense of
reverence for life, and faith in the potential of all people. They

emphasize self-actualization rather than self-sacrifice. Ultimately, they form the basis of the cocreative society — the societal butterfly.

WHEEL OF COCREATION WITH GOLDEN INNOVATIONS

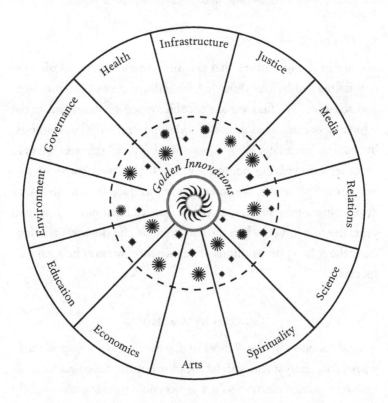

Criteria for golden innovations have been developed by LeCain and Mark Donohue.[6] The first three are subjective and qualitative. The others are quantitative and measurable.

1.   The innovation moves society toward the goal of a just, humane, regenerative, and choiceful future — the evolutionary agenda.

2. It comprises core values of the new paradigm that embody higher consciousness, greater freedom, and more synergistic order. These values include integrity, sustainability, inclusivity, nonviolence, gender balance, and win-win solutions that foster freedom, personal responsibility, and respect for others and self.

3. It has the potential for major social impact; it is more than a good project — it is one that can assist in the positive transformation of a vital function in the social body.

4. Its success is measurable, and it has achieved better quantifiable results than the majority of other approaches in comparable fields of endeavor.

5. It is more cost effective than other approaches over the long term and ideally also in the short term.

6. It has at least a two-year track record.

7. It is sustainable, replicable, and not dependent on one charismatic leader or other unique circumstances for its success.

As the Wheel is developed, examples of golden innovations will be found in every sector of the Wheel. Each embodies a story of dedication and love; each is a gift of creative action from heroes and heroines often unseen and unknown. These social entrepreneurs are people whose creativity and drive open major new possibilities in education, health, the environment, and other areas of human need. Just as business entrepreneurs lead innovation in commerce, social entrepreneurs drive social change. A new internet repository will host these golden innovations and the community that springs up around them.

To paint a picture of what is already emerging everywhere, I mention here a couple of social projects among the scores that are waiting to find their places within the process of transformation embodied in each sector of the Wheel.

Ashoka

Ashoka is a world fellowship that provides the foundation for pattern-changing visionaries who are alone in the newness of their works. Ashoka's network helps these visionaries, called Fellows, to find and help each other by sharing their professional experiences and methodologies. Founded by William Drayton in 1981, Ashoka encourages and assists individuals in making important innovations for the public good and builds an active mutual help fellowship among such public service entrepreneurs, both established and beginning, across all barriers. Ashoka has sought out and elected into its fellowship nearly eight hundred Fellows from Asia, Africa, Latin America, and central Europe. The criteria for being selected to receive an Ashoka fellowship are the following:

- The Knockout Test (A New Idea): Does this person have a truly new idea for solving a social problem?
- Creativity: Is he or she creative both in vision and goal setting and in problem solving?
- Entrepreneurial Quality: Is it impossible for this person to rest until his or her vision is the new pattern across society, even if it will likely involve years of relentless grappling with myriad how-to issues?
- Social Impact of the Idea: Is the idea itself sufficiently new, practical, and useful that ordinary people will adopt it after it has been demonstrated? Will it change the field significantly and trigger nationwide or broader regional change? How important is it and how beneficially will people be affected?
- Ethical Fiber: If the entrepreneur is not trusted, the likelihood of success is significantly reduced. The essential question is, "Do you trust this person [the fellowship candidate] absolutely?"

These criteria are useful for evaluating other golden innovations as well.

APPRECIATIVE INQUIRY

Based on similar successful principles of empowerment through positive affirmation, David L. Cooperrider, associate professor of Organizational Behavior at Case Western Reserve University, has developed a powerful social innovation for organizational development and transformation called appreciative inquiry — an inquiry into what we appreciate, affirm, and desire to cocreate in our future. He wrote in a paper titled "Appreciative Inquiry: A Constructive Approach to Organizational Development and Change":

> We have reached the "end of problem solving" as a mode of inquiry capable of inspiring, mobilizing, and sustaining human system change. The future of organizational development belongs to methods that affirm, compel, and accelerate anticipatory learning involving larger and larger levels of collectivity. The new methods will be distinguished by the art and the science of asking powerful, positive questions. The new methods will view realities as socially constructed and will therefore become more radically relational, widening the circle of dialogue to groups of 100s, 1000s, and perhaps more — with cyberspace relationships into the millions.... The arduous tasks of intervention will give way to the speed of imagination and innovation; and instead of negation, criticism, and spiraling diagnosis, there will be discovery, dream, design, and destiny.[7]

Can you imagine appreciative inquiries concerning what works on the internet involving millions of people? Is this not a potentially fundamental innovation leading toward the next stage of self-organization and democracy?

These examples and thousands more are based on faith in the goodness of human nature when we are placed in win-win social systems that bring out the best in us. Although a low-synergy, win-lose situation tends to bring out our worst traits, a win-win, high-synergy social system brings out our creativity and responsibility. As Maslow and the human potential movement affirmed the innate goodness of people, so these social innovations affirm the design systems that call forth our better nature in groups and in community. Imagine a continuous flow of such golden innovations entering the Wheel in each sector of the living system. It is the new body politic coming alive.

Global Cocreators

How will we locate golden innovations? How can we be assured that the new websites that connect conscious evolutionaries and track and activate global innovation will gather into the global brain and heart projects now changing the world for the good? The Global Cocreators are fulfilling this promise for us. They are an ever-expanding self-selected network of individuals now working to heal and evolve our world. Knowledgeable about innovations in their fields. they help identify breakthroughs and systemic changes. They evaluate, select, foster, nurture, and study innovations that work. Inspired to faithfully map and track the emerging integral culture, they work together to present information and ideas worldwide, just as people now do for Wikipedia.

Many such people already have highly developed websites, extended networks, and wide arenas of influence at the growing edge of change. Because of the rapid rise of the internet, the number of websites working on aspects of this new function is mounting daily. Since I started my campaign for a positive future, this meme has taken firm root. Here are some examples.

- Jerome C. Glenn, director of the Millennium Project (www.themp.org), has been connecting futurists around the world to improve global foresight since 1996. The project's fifty nodes (groups of individuals and institutions around the world) connect global and local perspectives to help people think together about the future to improve decisions today. Glenn also leads the Global Futures Intelligence System, an ongoing global network "functioning as a think tank on behalf of humanity, not on behalf of a government, an issue, or an ideology."[8]

- Eleanor LeCain, a leader in transformational politics, helps shine a light on what is working in her book *Breakthrough Solutions: How to Improve Your Life and Change the World by Building on What Works*.[9]

- Daniel Pinchbeck has cocreated the Center for Planetary Culture (www.planetaryculture.com), which includes the Regenerative Society wiki, in which people collaborate to present ideas in three main areas: technical infrastructure; social (political and economic) structure; and consciousness and culture, or superstructure.

- Corinne McLaughlin, with Gordon Davidson, has written *The Practical Visionary: A New World Guide to Spiritual and Social Change*, which presents eight keys to spiritual growth and social change.[10]

- In *Abundance: The Future Is Better Than You Think*, Peter H. Diamandis and Steven Kotler describe the improvement of society that is actually happening now.

- The Wisdom 2.0 conferences (www.wisdom2summit .com) invite participants to discuss how to use technology in ways that are useful to the world.

- The Emergence Project (www.theemergenceproject.net) is bringing together some of the world's leading thinkers to collectively develop a comprehensive "blueprint" for the future of humanity.

As demonstrated by these initiatives and countless more, this is not a dream of the future. Good works are arising everywhere, because good *works!* Those innovations that follow the general tendency toward sustainability and cocreativity are effective. People naturally seek to connect golden innovations working toward higher consciousness, freedom, and order. Their work together is vital for catalyzing our "global moon shot," which calls for rapid connectivity among separate innovations now working.

A Rising Tide

Just imagine major innovators coming together to identify golden innovations and to connect their innovations within the Wheel of Cocreation to represent a whole-system shift. We are now at the threshold of the most dynamic moment in history when we can join together to facilitate the gentle repatterning of our society.

Mappers would identify dozens of leading organizations, each expert in tracking social innovations, including the following:

- The Nobel Prize Committee, the MacArthur Foundation, and the Kyoto Prize, which separately recognize breakthroughs in the fields of peace, science, social innovation, and more
- Civicus, the largest mapper of civil society's successes
- The Social Venture Network, the leading global organization tracking and representing socially responsible businesses
- The Arias Foundation and Carter Center, which monitor conflict-resolution and disarmament initiatives
- Hazel Henderson's Ethical Markets Media (www.ethical

markets.com), which continually tracks ethical businesses worldwide

- The World Business Academy (www.worldbusiness.org), led by Rinaldo Brutoco, which unites business leaders concerned with the whole of society

This process would connect the most advanced resources and examples of where human innovation, aspiration, and perspiration are positively transforming the world. We would do much more than network, synergistically working on bringing forth a global database of the most exciting projects in human endeavor.

Social progress can no longer be engineered solely through large bureaucracies or centralized management. Civil society is already taking its place as a dynamic partner in the new leadership, as the top-down systems fail to solve our problems — problems that were actually created by the pyramid of separation inherent in those systems.

Communities of Cocreators

Golden innovations and the ever-growing network of global cocreators form one vital aspect of the new social process. The dynamism and power of these innovators and builders of the new world come from their own genius as well as the support and contributions of the rest of us — you and I and everyone applying their talents toward conscious evolution through actions large and small.

As part of this new process, people everywhere would enter their projects into the Wheel of Cocreation at any stage of development, provided that they were in alignment with the core values of conscious evolution. For example, projects based in violence, racial or ethnic prejudice, or environmental destruction would not belong in the Wheel.

Even now project initiators are learning about golden innovations in their fields to obtain the best guidelines available for stimulating individual creativity. These links to already-existing website databases of the best practices in every sector, such as health, education, and environment, are beginning to serve as a great reservoir of existing knowledge of what works.

We needn't reinvent the wheel when we begin a new project. We are building on successes throughout the system, but this process needs to be accelerated. For example, if there is a breakthrough in our scientific laboratories, it is quickly communicated to other scientists around the world. Yet in the realm of social innovations there is no comparable process. In fact, many people in the same town where a breakthrough innovation exists often don't know of the progress in their midst.

Compiling the countless projects into the Wheel of Cocreation would represent a "whole-system" shift. It would offer a holistic social architecture rather than the top-down model. Through this process, we would be able to study the patterns of success, the people, criteria, experiences, and circumstances now working toward the world we choose. The essence of the collaboration processes inspired by the worldview of conscious evolution is to build greater coherence and alignment within the peaks of our accumulated knowledge through the conscious connecting of the converging elements. This process will follow in the model Prigogine brought forth, whereby living systems "escape" into higher order and greater freedom through the increased interaction among innovations, as mentioned before.

As Maslow began the human potential movement by studying healthy people, we can now further empower the social potential movement by learning from, connecting, and amplifying healthy social innovations, continually building upon what works.

While our online platforms and social networks can help create community, global cocreators are also coming together in conferences of all kinds. It's important that we continue to listen carefully to one another, to seek the metapattern that connects,

COMMUNITY OF COCREATORS

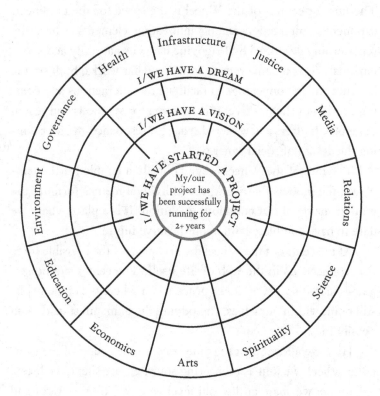

and to help discover the design of evolution for further communication and study. Beyond policy proposals, political platforms, and ideology-based solutions, we can create a blueprint based on pragmatic success in each functional area of the emerging society. Symbolically, it will represent a planetary DNA or memetic code of the next development of the social body. This ever-evolving design should be communicated as widely as possible.

As people from all over the world begin their projects, look for common goals, match needs and resources, connect with others, and dialogue with one another, the community of cocreators continues to develop.

Spirit at the Center

The hub, or center, of the Wheel is the space for the nonlinear, exponential interaction among innovating elements, where the repatterning described by Prigogine happens naturally and spontaneously. It is a convergence zone for what works, both on the internet and in convenings to facilitate the interactions and communication of the positive. It is an arena for synthesis and fusion of genius. It offers a new sacred space for resonance and for divining the design of social synergy.

The hub of the Wheel is symbolically a temple for the templates, the models that work, the individual memes forming the mother meme of our conscious evolution. It is a place where we dare to have complete faith in our positive future.

At the center of the Wheel dwells Spirit — the invisible force that connects us in the web of life itself. The center symbolizes a new sacred space, an inner peace room where we come to the still point within ourselves, embodying the unmanifest field of all possibilities.

Here we allow Spirit to connect us. In the center of the symbolic Wheel, we join as pioneering souls; we are silent, we listen, we attune; we share at the soul level what we know is right and good. We see how we can better coordinate our acts with others and with the larger process of creation.

The center of the Wheel is seen symbolically as a place in consciousness where the accumulated wisdom of the whole process of creation is focused and becomes conscious in us.

The Design of Evolution: The Evolutionary Spiral and the Wheel of Cocreation

In the illustration on page 165, we have paired the Wheel of Cocreation with the Evolutionary Spiral (see chapter 3) to represent three functions vital to catalyzing the once-in-a-civilization opportunity we are experiencing now. First, the Spiral and the

Wheel of Cocreation reveal a visual design of the universal story of creation, from the big bang to our turn on the Spiral. They give evolutionary meaning to the social potential movement by graphically representing our place in the context of the whole process of evolution.

Second, the Wheel of Cocreation, with its twelve functional sectors, seen as parts of the whole, offers us a pattern and a cocreative convergence process to cultivate social synergy. It invites us to connect what works in communities and virtually worldwide in the context of the evolutionary process.

Third, the hub at the center of the Wheel provides us with a new sacred space to cultivate resonance, revelation, and inspiration guided by the impulse of creation that runs through the whole Spiral.

The Spiral and the Wheel make the invisible patterns visible and useful to us all.

The Spiral represents the 13.8 billion years of evolution, flaring forth from the infinite, the mind of God.

The Core of the Spiral signifies Spirit in action, the impulse of evolution, the process of creation leading to higher consciousness, freedom, and order.

The Hub of the Wheel is where Source, Spirit, the impulse of evolution comes through each of us as we connect heart with heart. Imagine yourself within this new sacred space of evolution in resonance with two or more other people. It is a new "field" where you can join in small or large groups to feel connected, to love, to explore together the next stage of your own life in relationship to the emerging world.

The Communion of Pioneering Souls is symbolically a ring around the sacred space of the hub of the Wheel where we connect through the heart with everyone we love, and everyone they love, reaching out to connect with pioneering souls throughout the world.

The Planetary DNA is where we come together to divine the design of the cocreative culture emerging in our midst. It is the space where we discover the emerging pattern of the whole.

The Sectors of the Wheel are twelve societal disciplines or functions basic to any community. Just as your body has various organs and parts that perform vital functions — the heart, the liver, the brain, the legs, and so on — so does the planetary body. Each of us is a cell in the larger body with a unique part to play in one or more sectors of the Wheel. The twelve-around-one model is the basis of the concept of tensegrity pioneered by Buckminster Fuller. It is the most stable form in nature. It is the pattern that holds the separate parts together in a new union far greater than the sum of the parts, as in our own physical bodies with fifty trillion cells!

The Golden Innovations are projects in every sector of society that work toward a cocreative world. Nature always selects for what works. To see the pattern of evolution, we connect innovations, solutions, and breakthroughs now working toward a sustainable world. That's where we find that we have the capacity to feed, house, clothe, and care for all of us.

Global Cocreators are social innovators, masters in every field, in every culture. Every community is filled with gifted people. They need to be invited in, honored, connected, celebrated, and learned from, community by community, until we have a global field of wisdom and brilliance. These individuals join together to form communities of cocreators, connecting with one another worldwide to work on projects in every sector of the Wheel. We are a mighty force never before assembled.

We can see the Wheel as a process of convergence representing our turn on the Spiral and each of us liberated to express our creativity within the whole, leading toward endless evolutionary transformation, beyond us, in this universe without end.

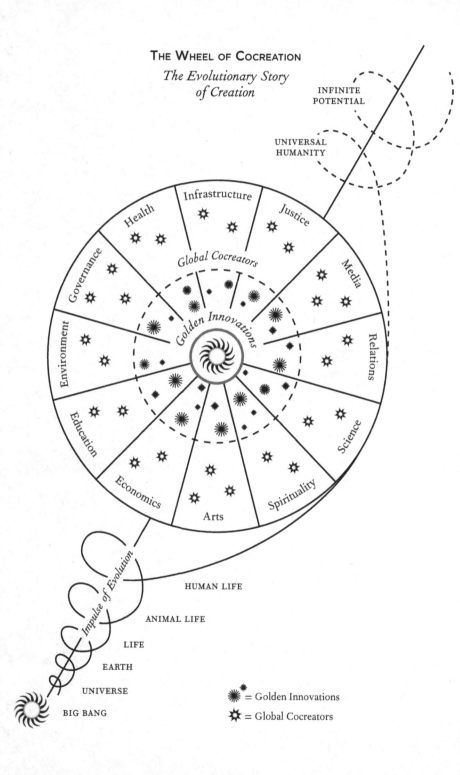

THE WHEEL OF COCREATION

*The Evolutionary Story
of Creation*

INFINITE
POTENTIAL

UNIVERSAL
HUMANITY

Infrastructure

Health

Justice

Governance

Global Cocreators

Media

Environment

Golden Innovations

Relations

Education

Science

Economics

Spirituality

Arts

Impulse of Evolution

HUMAN LIFE

ANIMAL LIFE

LIFE

EARTH

UNIVERSE

BIG BANG

✳ = Golden Innovations

✵ = Global Cocreators

CHAPTER TWELVE

A Pattern of
Transformation Revealed

Prigogine described how nature has evolved from simplicity to greater complexity through (among other factors) the increased and novel interactions within a highly nonequilibrium system, resulting in a quantum jump, a repatterning to a higher order. The new social function we are describing will facilitate our social system to make such a jump through providing the opportunity for greater and more coherent interactions among innovating elements.

As we have seen, our global society can be viewed as a large dissipative structure that is increasingly undergoing perturbations. On the one hand, there is an acceleration of breakdowns. On the other hand, breakthroughs are arising everywhere. We can see that every sector of the Wheel of Cocreation is actually a strand of the evolutionary agenda that is part of a whole system.

The acceleration of breakdowns in our system, such as population growth, hunger, poverty, violence, environmental decay, resource shortages, species extinction, toxic wastes, the greenhouse effect, and pollution of the seas and the soil, accelerated now by climate change, are mutually interactive. They are leading to increased entropy and danger that may cause irreversible damage to our life system in a very short period of time.

What is almost never noticed, however, is that there is a concurrent convergence of positive social innovations. It is a matter of timing as to which happens first: the exponential convergence of the breakdowns or the breakthroughs (which will become critical and cause the quantum change). Will we go downward toward devolution or upward toward evolutionary transformation and metamorphosis?

If the positive innovations connect exponentially before the massive breakdowns reinforce one another, as suggested by the idea of the "global moon shot," the system can repattern itself to a higher order of consciousness and freedom without the predicted economic, environmental, or social collapse. Can we evolve toward the positive as quickly as we might devolve toward the negative? Are we in one of those moments of evolutionary quantum change? During these moments of radical change doing more of the same will not work. What needs to happen is social synergy — the phenomenon of nonlinear exponential interactions of projects that work. This is the call to the spirit-motivated process of action. It could make the critical difference between a quantum jump to syntropy, cooperation, and cocreation or to entropy, conflict, devaluation, and chaos. If the system could go either way, a slight intervention to assist the convergence of the positive can tip the scales of evolution in favor of the enhancement of life on Earth.

We need to facilitate what is natural but is being restricted by divisiveness in our system, such as the separation between all disciplines, the competition and violence among religions and nations, the mass media's emphasis on breakdowns, and the absence of a cooperative, cocreative process within and among organizational structures.

Where We Are Now

We are in a period of dramatic increased instability, confusion, loss of vision. Tension is increasing everywhere as the old order struggles to prevail and the new order tries to emerge; we are in what may be called the "tension zone." Innovators run into complexities and difficulties, both in the external world through resistant social systems and through immaturities, addictions, and egotism within themselves.

As the climb gets steeper, any flaws in our character will show up. To enter the convergence zone as those who are responsible for social innovations, we must become mature imaginal cells. It is a time for continued self-development as we realize that we are not only intending to heal what is sick but to evolve what is well. In fact, the social potential movement gives new meaning to the effort of millions within the human potential movement. The "self-actualizing society" is the fulfillment of the rising numbers of self-actualizing people. To take the next step, we are becoming ever more conscious of our own state of being — of our thoughts and intentions. For as we approach the convergence zone, everything within us is magnified, our weaknesses as well as our strengths. The pressure on all social change agents is intense. We continue to struggle to evolve — personally, financially, organizationally — usually with little support from our current culture. Many of us may fall by the wayside, at least for the moment. But those who persevere through the tension zone have a great reward in store for them. For inside the convergence zone, new patterns prevail and reinforce one another, synchronicities increase, and we get a taste of the cocreative society — heaven on Earth.

Practicing the personal path of the cocreator is vital, for it helps us stabilize our own higher internal consciousness so that we can remain at a high enough frequency or state of being to resonate with the energy within the convergence zone. Most particularly, we seek to overcome our ego-driven behavior — our desire to dominate and win over others — and learn to cooperate and cocreate. Few of us have learned to remain in our higher state of being. We are competitive and have a desire to win. We lose resonance, we fear rejection, judgment seeps in, and we fall into separation — then struggle to rise again and again, seeking to stabilize. Very few of us have stabilized at our own high norm (certainly including me). We flicker in and out of higher consciousness. But remember, we are still a young species. We have not yet discovered what it means to be fully human. This is the work of the maturing social potential movement: to provide win-win social systems within which the higher qualities of love, creativity, and the responsibility of humanity can be reinforced and secured.

The Joys of Cocreation

When we enter the convergence zone, our new state of being as cocreators is enhanced and stabilized. We experience the joys of cocreation. We have all felt this magnificent state in flashes of peak experiences, when we are in the zone, in the swing of things. It occurs whenever two or more pioneering souls are drawn together to cocreate, to fuse genius, to work on an activity that actualizes each person's unique potential. In those moments we experience resonance, a re-sounding, or echoing, of each other's higher qualities. This wonderful feeling affirms and reinforces each person's creativity.

Mihaly Csikszentmihalyi in *The Evolving Self* refers to this state as "flow" and defines it as when we are using all our capacities to realize a goal of intrinsic value:

Flow usually occurs when there are clear goals a person tries to reach and when there is unambiguous feedback as to how well he or she is doing.... When we enjoy it, it is because we think of it as something that allows us to express our potential, to learn about our limits, to stretch our being. It is for this reason that flow is such an important force in evolution. Without it, our genetic programs would instruct us to continue pursuing what has been "good for us" in the past; but flow makes us receptive to the entire world as a source of new challenges, as an arena for creativity.... It is an escape forward into higher complexity, where one hones one's potential by confronting new challenges. Because the fine balance between challenge and skill makes it necessary to concentrate on the task at hand, people in flow report a loss of self-consciousness.[1]

In other words, the experience of separateness and awareness of self as a separate being dissolves in the flow state. A more unitive form of consciousness is momentarily achieved.

Dissonance and resistance dissolve when we fuse our genius. Convergence "eats" entropy. Two or more gathered in resonance in evolutionary circles form basic building blocks of the integral culture. In this field of resonance, our self-expression is amplified and flows naturally. Nature has built in an incentive for cocreation just as she has for procreation. It is pleasure! In the convergence zone, we do not solve our problems in the same state of consciousness in which we created them. For in the process of coming together to solve problems, we ourselves are changed, our genius codes join, and something greater than ourselves emerges from our union with other kindred souls. That is, love!

The Four Ss

When we are in the convergence zone, the Four Ss prevail: synergy, synchronicity, syntony, and suprasex. The joy intensifies, we feel social ease, laughter, fun, and effortlessness. That's how we can tell we are in the "zone." Let's see what the Four Ss teach us.

1. SYNERGY

Synergy is the experience that we are part of a larger group or social body. It is the glorious sense of becoming ourselves more fully through deeper participation with others. In a synergistic team, all we need to do is our part and allow and encourage others to do their parts. Our part becomes amplified and fulfilled through joining with others, who are experiencing the same fulfillment of their unique parts through joining with us. The words "love your neighbor as yourself" become a reality. The "other" is part of oneself. In synergy we recognize that we are members of a larger whole; the dichotomy between self and other is overcome. The illusion of separation dissolves as the uniqueness of each person increases through participation in the greater whole.

By the alignment among all members of the body, the binding force of nature, grace, Spirit — whatever name we call it — joins us as part of a larger whole in which we, as separate parts, mysteriously feel more uniquely ourselves than ever before. The word "cooperation" changes its meaning from helping one another to being members of one body coordinated by the larger process of creation.

2. SYNCHRONICITY

Carl Jung defined it in *Synchronicity: An Acausal Connecting Principle* as "a meaningful coincidence of two or more events, where something other than the probability of chance is involved."[2] In the convergence zone, synchronicities increase. The timing is not in our hands; events seem to occur as needed. Complexities that could not be planned for appear to self-organize. There is a sense of effortlessness although everyone is working very hard.

People we are looking for are often looking for us. We ask a question and the answer comes quickly, often in strange and unexpected ways. When we are in the flow there is the feeling of being organized by the deeper pattern rather than by having to make things happen by will and linear planning alone. We still plan and execute, but with a feeling of grace and support rather than by will alone. We sense we are coordinated by the whole of which we are a part. This feeling may be accurate, for in the flow state we are more sensitive to the deeper tendency in evolution toward higher consciousness and greater freedom.

3. SYNTONY

This term, coined by Erich Jantsch in his book *Design for Evolution*, described one of the ways of accessing conscious evolution, as mentioned earlier.[3] The relationship between the cosmic design and the individual intensifies through some form of syntony or resonance. Syntony feels like guidance, intuition, or direct knowing. We do not have to figure out what to do. We know. We perform with spontaneous right action. The inner world of subjective experience and the outer world of objective reality blend and become one. We and the world "outside us" are interconnected in one larger field of intelligence. The great flashes of awareness that mystics have experienced throughout history are reinforced and normalized. Each of us becomes more attuned to the deeper patterns; intuition and intellect blend. The mystical state becomes grounded and manifested in spirit-motivated social action.

4. Suprasex

The next stage of sexuality, suprasex, occurs when our genius is aroused and we desire to join our genius to cocreate. Suprasexual passion increases in the convergence zone. We are vocationally aroused at the level of our genius. Instead of joining our genes to have a child, we yearn to join our genius to give birth to our full potential selves and to the creativity that expresses our combined love. Energy floods into our systems. Procreation extends itself into cocreation. We do not tire as easily or get sick as often. We feel exhilarated, lighthearted, and exuberant. Brilliant ideas are triggered by the presence of others who reinforce our own potential. Even our sexuality is enhanced, not to have a child but to "have ourselves," to regenerate ourselves through love. While the emphasis is not on sexuality but on creativity, sexuality *is* enhanced by suprasex and by vocational arousal. We're excited. It's fun! In fact, for many of us as we live longer lives, this new passion is *the* most rewarding and loving part of our lives. It's the reason for longevity and extended health.

Possessiveness and self-centeredness dissolve for the moment, not out of self-sacrifice, but out of self-fulfillment through cocreation. The ego is absorbed through expressing its uniqueness. The poison of selfishness is dissolved as we give our best in such a way that both we as individuals and as others are blessed by our creativity.

In certain moments of convergence, we experience the ecstasy of cocreation. It feels as though we are one with the creative impulse within ourselves and our partners, which transcends the self-centered individual. In the act of expressing our genius and of being received in love by other members of the whole, we feel as though we've come home at last, no longer alien and cast out in unfamiliar surroundings, as we give of ourselves lovingly and we are received in love. This is a form of "social love" possible in a cocreative world. It combines "eros," erotic love, and "agape," altruistic love, arousing our passion at all levels of being. Another word for this kind of love is "telerotic." "Telos" means "higher purpose," and "eros" is "passionate love." When passionate lovers join for higher purpose, they become telerotic!

Stabilizing the Experience of Cocreation

At our current stage of evolution, we are deeply drawn to stabilize the experience, not as an ecstatic high but as a new normalcy. We proceed by making normal what was first a peak experience. The pleasure principle is intrinsic to social evolution. We do not evolve the world by guilt and duty any more than we populated the world through such feelings!

Our social structures often separate us, keeping us from our natural desire to cocreate. We simply haven't known that social convergence is the key to our heart's desire. We are separated into disciplines, fields, mind-sets, ideologies, colors, races, economic classes, and religions. Our communities and families are breaking apart, and we are often lonely, isolated, and purposeless. For lack of something exciting to attract us forward, many of us are looking backward to our ethnic roots for exclusive identity, or sinking into the misery of substance abuse, depression, illness, even violence and despair. We have not created systems to help us find our teammates, partners, and social cocreators at local or regional levels. Few places are designed specifically for joining our genius and giving birth to our projects and gifts to the world.

Yet we can see that the process of evolution tends to favor our higher consciousness, our greater freedom, and our efforts toward a win-win synergistic society. Every such intention and action is reinforced by the tendency in evolution that has been moving forward toward greater complexity for billions of years. Although there is freedom in the system, and increasingly so, it is also true that the universe is designed to select and enhance higher states of being and doing, as it has demonstrated in the progression from molecule to cell to animal to human to the great avatars, and now to us attempting to become a universal, cocreative species. From the perspective of conscious evolution, we are not operating in a vacuum or in a neutral universe, but in a universal living system animated everywhere with intelligence, growing toward higher consciousness and freedom. It is this intelligence that we are becoming aware of in us, as us, as we practice our own conscious evolution.

Our passion to create and self-express is always driving us toward convergence. The drives for self-preservation and self-reproduction are merging into Maslow's second drive — self-actualization — giving us the fuel to forge the evolutionary frontier. In the United States, for example, we invented the Constitution, the jury, the vote, the town meeting, and the Bill of Rights for the first phase of freedom, and now we are inventing a new social architecture for cocreation.

SYNCON

In my experience, one of the very best ways of cultivating social synergy is the SYNCON process. SYNCON stands for "synergistic convergence," and the process brings people together locally to share their passions, to match their needs and resources, and to optimally cocreate. It changes the social architecture from the pyramidal, top-down structure of modern civilization to the integrative, whole-system structure of circles, based on the Wheel of Cocreation.

My Committee for the Future in Washington, DC, in the 1970s developed twenty-five SYNCON Conferences, which took place in wheel-shaped environments, a local version of the Wheel of Cocreation, to bring diverse and opposing people together to seek common goals and match needs with resources. It was the Wheel of Cocreation come alive. Everyone was asked three questions: What do you want to create? What do you need to create it? What resources do you want to share freely? People sought common goals and matched needs with resources throughout the group. At the end, we took "all walls down," removing the portable walls that divided the Wheel's sectors, so that we could sense ourselves as a whole social body.

At every conference, people discovered they could better achieve what they wanted through cocreation rather than opposition. Synergy creates more energy. The social whole is greater than the sum of its parts. And connecting to cocreate is a form of social love.

Many other groups have reported that using the SYNCON process and the Wheel of Cocreation has helped them create positive social change. For example, the Hague Center for Innovation, Global Governance, and Emergence (www.thehague center.org) is currently activating the architecture of the Wheel of Cocreation to bring communities in Monterrey, Mexico, and Cairo, Egypt, into transformative change processes. They report that the process allows them to create the necessary conditions for the emergence of resilient and thriving communities with more evolved governance models, social cohesion, and spiritual awareness. Kimberly and Foster Gamble are also using the Wheel of Cocreation to great benefit in their work with the Thrive Movement (www.thrivemovement.com).

How to Do a SYNCON

SYNCON works with groups from twenty-five to several hundred people. The process is very simple and can be done in person, online, or both.

It is advisable to use the illustrations of the Spiral and the

Wheel of Cocreation upon which the SYNCON model is built. Anyone who is coordinating the process can offer the context and perspective of the 13.8 billion years of history leading up to this moment, as well as the simple lessons of evolution, such as the fact that problems are evolutionary drivers. This context is very helpful and exciting for the process of synergistic convergence.

The SYNCON process is as follows:

1. People meet in each sector of the Wheel according to their functional interests and vocational calling, forming a "task force" in each sector. (The Wheel categories discussed in this book may be used, or others may be devised as needed.) Participants form one or more circles in each sector of the Wheel. A scribe, a facilitator, and a spokesperson from each sector volunteer to represent that task force.

2. Each member of the circle responds to three questions:
   - What is my passion to create now?
   - To fulfill this desire, what do I need that I do not now have — what is lacking?
   - What resources do I have to give to this group or to people in other sectors of the social body?

3. After listening carefully to one another, participants form smaller groups based on shared purpose and affinity. They support one another and often devise joint plans.

4. The smaller groups reassemble in their sector of the Wheel and share their joint strategies.

5. Each sector prepares a composite statement of goals, needs, and resources.

6. The whole group meets in an Assembly of the Whole. The assembly can be visually exciting, in theater-in-the-round style, with ribbon dividers, placards, or artistic

renditions to suggest the different functions of the social body.

7. Each task force's spokesperson presents the shared statement of goals, needs, and resources of its group to the Assembly of the Whole. Everyone listens actively to each presentation, noting where one group's needs and another's resources match. Each sector chooses from among its members "vocational ambassadors" to visit other sectors.

8. A facilitated mingling occurs, either of functional sectors or of individuals and groups, seeking the synergies, linkages, and connections that are natural to any system but are often unnoticed because the process does not facilitate their discovery. If a video camera is available, it becomes the "nervous system" of the group. People call for the camera whenever they have a breakthrough or new linkage. The Four Ss — synergy, synchronicity, syntony, and suprasex (see page 172) — are cultivated. If possible, a NewNews show (as described in chapter 13) is edited from the event, expressing the fact that cocreating is the news now, fostering the social uprising of wellness.

9. The Assembly of the Whole reassembles. Each group re-presents its goals, needs, and resources, taking into account expanded connections and synergies. According to the time available, the assembly can discover more synergies and experience the fact that the whole is greater than the sum of its parts. Participants find they are better able to achieve their goals through cocreation than through adversarial or even competitive tactics. Music and dance can be used. In the end, a celebration occurs and people walk the Evolutionary Spiral together.

10. Ideally a local website is developed. Each task force is invited to place its goals, needs, and resources on the

website. Eventually, many such websites will connect to help people find common goals and match needs with resources throughout the system, as suggested in chapter 11. The NewNews coverage (see chapter 13) of these connections can be communicated via email, websites, and other media.

SYNCON remains one of the best processes that we can apply at the local and global scales, as well as in face-to-face and virtual contexts. The SYNCON process can best be understood when seen as part of the whole story of creation, symbolized in the Spiral and the Wheel of Cocreation (see page 165).

CHAPTER THIRTEEN

The NewNews

Let's imagine that the social potential movement is emerging and gathering strength. Teams are forming to act as catalysts to help bring the process into focus. Now what is needed to make the system work is the maturation of our mass media, our planetary nervous system. We must see images of social wellness if we are to have the faith and courage to heal our society and grow. Imagine what would happen if a newborn child were surrounded only by people who thought it was ugly and who noticed only its weaknesses, messes, and failures. Think how the child would be affected. We are a newly emerged planetary society, and we need to make sure we are receiving positive feedback. We need an extraordinary media outreach that can set the new template and affect all other media.

The NewNews: Channels for Cocreation

The single most important thing we could do with the media is offer a new conception of what we mean by news. Many people believe what they see on the news is the truth. For this evolutionary plan to succeed we need to cocreate a prototype: the New-News. We have already envisioned the movement for what works spreading throughout the world via rapidly increasing networking among innovators. Now let's build on that and imagine a television show called *The NewNews: What's Working in the World*. It is real "tell-a-vision" but also available on the internet and radio, or it might even start on the internet. It is a megaphone for creative breakthroughs and successes, which invites millions of people to participate in constructive action.

The NewNews is the real-life drama of the human family's struggle to evolve. I can imagine it taking place in a new kind of live "situation room" fed by golden innovations streaming in through all types of media that are reporting good news and good works. The feeling in such NewNews rooms is one of genuine excitement, danger, and opportunity, because the real question is, Evolution or extinction? Will we make it through this critical period or won't we? Initiators and innovators are seen as genuine heroes and heroines, the true newsmakers of our time. The New-News invites all of us to start on the hero's path. It acknowledges that we are on a hero's journey together.

Guests come on the show to report what's working. Every innovator who speaks of a project that works is asked to share how it works and why it works — to help others achieve similar successes. Golden innovations are dramatized, especially from the personal point of view. How did you do it? How did your family respond? How did you support yourself? Where did you suffer? What did you enjoy? We learn from one another how to be innovators. Imagine our visions and our social goals in a segment on the NewNews entitled "Visions of a Positive Future." People are invited to communicate their visions of the emerging world so that tell-a-vision can collect them and continually report to viewers the future they are choosing to create. Remember *conscious evolution* means evolution by choice, not chance.

The NewNews also addresses the challenges we are facing. It tells the stories of the breakdowns and disasters in terms of the vital question of what people can do to help. Each breakdown is seen in its dramatic context, as a problem that is an evolutionary driver, pressing us toward something better and more creative. The real drama of life in the twenty-first century is the heroic effort of millions of people to avoid disaster and foster emergence and innovation.

We use techniques similar to those David Ellis offered in his book, *Creating Your Future*, urging people to project into the long-range future to overcome self-imposed limitations.[1] We begin collectively to do what James Redfield described in *The Tenth Insight* and in *The Celestine Vision*.[2] We "hold the vision" built of all our choices, potentials, and pragmatic successes. By placing our ever-expanding and enriching vision on the news, we begin to see it as real and are thereby further activated to realize it now in our lives. It is not something in the future we are waiting for, but rather a stimulus to awaken our creativity in the present. What we envision we begin to create.

The hosts of the NewNews pay particular attention to reporting on situations in which adversaries begin to agree on something, for finding common ground is one of the foundational elements of the emerging culture. For example, I remember a specially designed SYNCON, or synergistic convergence conference, produced by the Committee for the Future, which we put on for gang leaders in the inner city of Los Angeles. (The Committee for the Future produced twenty-five such synergistic conferences from 1972 to 1976.) We gathered together the leading gangs of Los Angeles: Hispanic, Asian, African American, and white. The process was designed to have people state their passions to create their goals, needs, and resources, and to seek common goals in a wheel-shaped environment divided into sectors, as in the Wheel of Cocreation. The police, welfare recipients, former convicts, shopkeepers, crime victims, corporate executives, and science fiction writers like Ray Bradbury and Gene Roddenberry were also present.

At one point we felt a sense of something new and fragile coming together. Each task force stated its goals, what it needed to accomplish the goals, and the resources it could offer to others. The police and corporate executives were paying close attention to the kids' words. All participants met as equal members of the community trying to work out something together. One black gang leader was standing in the center of the circle in his worn leather jacket. He had been quiet and looked depressed throughout the three-day event. Suddenly he took a deep breath and spoke in a voice so soft that all of us had to lean toward him to hear. "I think it's going to be all right, we're going to be heard..." he said.

In that instant an ABC-TV camera crew arrived. They started to pull gang members aside to find out what was going on. The young black leader who had just spoken faced the TV cameras and said loudly for all to hear: "Go away! We won't let you do this to us again. We won't let you make us look bad. Go away!"

The mass media cameras retreated, our little handheld camera zoomed in on the young man, and we heard his story, for the first time, of how the media had distorted gangs by always communicating their worst behavior. We began to discuss important issues with the members of those gangs. It was a very powerful and moving experience as they started to communicate. My partner at the time, the late John Whiteside, created "The New World Evening News," in which he played back the peaks of new agreements and acts of cooperation that occurred on that day. People were fascinated to see themselves as newsmakers and wanted to watch the program over and over. "The New World Evening News" format and approach can be incorporated into the NewNews.

A major twenty-four-hour-a-day "human potential television" channel may not be that far from manifestation. It would have programming focusing on such themes as living as a whole person, lifelong learning, personal growth, vocational development, spirituality, what's working to create a better world, and personal stories of our new leaders in progress.

On December 22, 2012, I coproduced (with Stephen Dinan, CEO of The Shift Network) Birth 2012, a coordinated series of events in countries all over the world (for more on Birth 2012, see page 221). We were able to use the internet and Maestro Conference telephone technology to create a channel where, for twenty-four hours, we spread the good news of what was happening around the globe to birth our new planetary consciousness. We had videographers reporting in from many regions of the world. It was an amazing experience to see in real time the response to our announcement of the planetary birth.

This and other such efforts are favorably disposed to the NewNews idea. It is only a matter of time, energy, and focus to make it happen at a comprehensive and popular scale required to reach the general public.

Another powerful form of media is the arts. Artists are essential to the NewNews — to inspire, reveal, and illuminate what is happening. Poets, dancers, painters, and musicians weave a web of meaning and revelation throughout the NewNews show. Earl Hubbard's statement made so long ago in the little café on the Left Bank — "we need artists to tell us our new story" — comes true on the NewNews. We find creative talent that has been blocked from expression by the limited access and negative self-image prevalent in popular culture. Our birth as universal humanity calls forth an outpouring of creativity as our new self-images, visions, and dreams are portrayed by artistic genius.

Through the technology of computer animation, we have the breathtaking ability to dramatize and make our visions real. Seeing is believing. Advanced art forms are a vital part of cocreating the future.

Through the NewNews programming, viewers will be invited to turn on their computers and place their projects, their dreams, and their visions on websites that share and link to the NewNews. These websites should develop a service for matching needs with resources through a vocational dating service spotlighted by the NewNews. Suprasex will be encouraged! Examples of social love stories abound. People finding each other are turned on. "Telerotic" partners joined by shared purpose and juicy love will be invited to share stories, to tell of the fun they are having cocreating.

This matching function will help people find their teammates, their partners, and their projects, stirring the creative energy latent in millions. Imagine that vocational arousal sweeps the nation and the world, as the NewNews goes global. Imagine that local communities create their own NewNews channels on the internet. We could find ourselves in the midst of a social uprising of wellness.

What do you suppose will happen to most modern news shows when the NewNews becomes popular? They will start to compete. Reporters will be told to find out what's working. Muckrakers will become pearl-rakers. Yellow journalism will become silver and gold! People will start noticing what's working in their own lives. The NewNews will be flooded with stories of what works from all around the world.

The truth is that the NewNews is not far from being realized. Back in the 1990s, Peter Jennings, the anchor for ABC's national news, introduced into the evening news a segment called

"Solutions" that highlighted innovations and breakthroughs. In the United Kingdom, *Positive News* has since been established to report on positive developments from around the world.

Founded in 2013 by Foundation for Conscious Evolution board member Sandra de Castro Buffington, UCLA's Global Media Center for Social Impact (www.gmimpact.org) actively engages entertainment-industry leaders to create compelling story lines that accurately portray a wide range of socially provocative issues, including racial justice, LGBT rights, gender equality, immigration, health, climate change, prison reform, and the mind-body-spirit connection. The center harnesses the power of television, film, music, and new media so that exceptional storytelling, socially conscious songwriting, effective reporting, and interactive content on new media can move us from evidence to impact.

A truly global media is being created. But there are tremendous issues of credibility and responsibility that professional journalists, amateur journalists, bloggers, and even "accidental journalists" — people with smartphones in the right place at the right time — need to consider. How do we connect authentically? What is newsworthy? How do we cover important issues in a healthy, balanced way? How do we inspire, inform, and lead? This is where media literacy comes in. Media professional Cate Montana (www.catemontana.com) recommends two superb organizations that are creating a conversation around media literacy and all that it implies: Journalism That Matters (www.journalism thatmatters.net), and Images and Voices of Hope (www.IVOH .org). Welcome to the conversation!

Let's imagine the NewNews as popular TV shows in a variety of forms, broadcast worldwide and locally via the internet, radio, and TV. Situation comedies, dramas, and documentaries soon follow the news, revealing the numberless stories of the frontiers of human progress. Storytelling goes well beyond the news. When stories of conscious cocreation find their way into dramas, comedies, animated series, feature films, and songs, they can transport viewers into new worlds, become part of popular culture, and cocreate our future. The stories capture the imagination, and change attitudes, knowledge, and behavior in the process.

Everywhere communities are creating their own NewNews outlets, and individuals are calling in to NewNews outlets, asking how they can learn to be cocreators, how they can become social innovators, how they can help bring into being a better future. The stage is set for a new education in conscious evolution.

CHAPTER FOURTEEN

Education for Conscious Evolution

Education for conscious evolution is the context in which all disciplines and fields work together to understand and guide the evolution of humanity. It is the metadiscipline we need to provide the knowledge, motivation, and opportunities upon which leadership in this century will form.

Ralph Abraham, the renowned chaos theorist and mathematician, highlighted the necessity for an education in conscious evolution. In *Chaos, Gaia, Eros* he wrote:

> Here is the crux of the world problem. Its evolution — *cultural evolution*, or *sociogenesis* — is subject to the laws of general evolution theory. As we learn laws from comparative studies in the histories of geogenesis, biogenesis, and noogenesis, we may develop the capability to guide our own sociogenesis, and to participate in the creation of our future. This points to a new science of the future, a *true* social science, with mathematical models and

observational laws, with understanding and wisdom, and with a basis in history and social philosophy.[1]

As we have seen, the first part of the process is to understand our new story of creation and our new meme of conscious evolution. Then comes the formation of a new social architecture to facilitate the communication and convergence of positive actions. We have envisioned expanding processes of finding golden innovations and "what works," supported by vital platforms that scan for, map, connect, and communicate the most creative breakthroughs in every field. We envisioned global cocreators, masters in their fields, at every level — local, regional, and global — who are seeking out emergent potentials currently changing the system. They are piecing together an ever-evolving design for a positive future based on synergy among innovations. A vast community on the internet is participating in the discovery, empowerment, and replication of what is working in every field. And finally, we envisioned a continuing broadcasting of breakthroughs and successes over the NewNews to educate our society on the positive changes occurring — inviting public participation in what works. This process is the basis for a new education for conscious evolution.

Now, let's imagine that millions of people are inspired by what they see and hear is happening throughout the world and they want to participate. Where do people learn to be social innovators? Who can assist them in discovering their evolutionary vocations and in entering the lifelong learning process of cocreation?

In fifth-century Greece there was the agora — the marketplace of ideas, a popular assembly site where Socrates and Plato held their famous dialogues to challenge students' beliefs. The foundations of philosophy, ethics, and metaphysics were laid out. Later, in medieval times, universities emerged. They were great preservers and communicators of knowledge.

Our modern universities are still structured in the medieval model — divided into disciplines and fields — with scant integrative orientation to guide us to develop the visions, purposes, and goals of humanity as a whole entering the first age of conscious evolution. Many teachers and isolated curricula are occurring throughout society that offer aspects of conscious evolution. Workshops, seminars, and trainings proliferate. Yet, these brilliant educational initiatives are scattered, disconnected, and often unknown to students who want to learn. For all the experimentation in education, we are still limited to an antiquated educational framework that offers little relationship among disciplines and gives little opportunity for students to ask the ultimate questions about our destiny and how they can participate in creating a positive future.

As a young and unsuspecting imaginal cell, I had no idea of my vocation when I entered Bryn Mawr College; I looked at all the separate courses — English, history, science, art — each in an unrelated box, but couldn't relate the courses to my quest for life purpose. I did not know what I wanted to do or be. I had a slight glimmer, which most of us have, yet found no way to nourish my faint vision. I wrote in my journal for the first time in May 1948, when I was eighteen years old and a sophomore in college:

> I've waited far too long to begin my journal. Feelings, intuitions, ideas have been lost irrevocably. I have a desperate need to create. All my life I have absorbed. By using myself as a catalytic agent, I hope to give pattern and form to the mass of sensations that have impressed themselves upon me. The power of intelligence is to connect, to relate, and to integrate impressions. If there is a God, it is One who unites past with present and future, finite with infinite, truths with apparently conflicting truths, until all are more than a conglomeration, all is one and

that one is far greater than the sum of its parts. That one is God's creation.

Given the broad and undefined nature of my quest, how could I choose what to major in, much less what to minor in? There was nothing seemingly available to facilitate the discovery of my life purpose. There wasn't even a place to *ask the question* of the direction of human civilization and what might be my part in it.

My roommate, whom I had just met, suggested that we go to Washington to get a job after college. I agreed and therefore chose political science for my major. It was that haphazard.

You may say that my search for meaning was somewhat obsessive, but I believe we all have the same need to find what we are born to do and where we are needed to do it.

Eventually, as I found my vocation, my father would say, "Barbara, you're the best in the field — but there's no field!" Recently, Professor A. Harris Stone put it this way when he asked me to write a rationale for the new field of conscious evolution: "There is a body of knowledge, but there is no field." We need to establish this new field of thought so it can be introduced into the academic community as well as into the social and political communities, thus enabling proper research that will in turn make the body of knowledge accessible to the brightest minds of our time. But it is often difficult, if not impossible, to introduce something new into an old form. It is now time to bring together those who have the vision, and the passion, to develop the curriculum for conscious evolution. Even now many people are at work teaching, often hidden within more traditional systems. When the larger context is established to create a new educational system, these innovators will be ready to add to the curriculum for conscious evolution.

A Metadiscipline for the Twenty-First Century

Because all disciplines are needed to understand and guide ethical evolution, the commitment to conscious evolution will help us break out of the boxes of separate disciplines structured so deeply into our academic institutions. The metadiscipline of conscious evolution offers us a coherent matrix in which all our disciplines fit. The framework is the Evolutionary Spiral seen as the process of creation now continuing through us, in what Duane Elgin called a continuous creation — seeing our futures as a continuum of this process unfolding into an ever-expanding horizon of no known limits. All functions are interrelated, as in any living body. Through the metadiscipline of conscious evolution, we greatly enhance our understanding of how to cocreate new systems appropriate for this stage of evolution.

Cosmology, geology, anthropology, history, science and technology, psychology, art, current affairs, and futures are not separate subjects, but interrelated processes that have brought us to this point of evolution. In the context of conscious evolution students in the various disciplines would have to converge in an effort to understand how to evolve consciously. Gregory Bateson wrote in the introduction to *Mind and Nature: A Necessary Unity*, "What is the pattern which connects all the living creatures? ... The pattern which connects is a meta-pattern. It is a pattern of patterns."[2] It is this metapattern that the metadiscipline of education for conscious evolution seeks to understand and apply to guide our actions in the coming millennium.

New Schools and Programs
for Conscious Evolution

To house the new metadiscipline, new schools for conscious evolution are needed — not only schools of thought but also educational sites, whether in accredited universities or not, where people gather to teach and learn how to participate in conscious evolution, spiritually, socially, and scientifically. Online and face-to-face learning centers for conscious evolution will provide students (meaning all of us) with knowledge, connections, mentors, and skills needed to fulfill our vocations of destiny in the evolution of ourselves and the world. They will be places to stir the intellectual, social, and spiritual ferment needed for this quantum jump.

What we need now are educational programs, processes, and courses on conscious evolution to facilitate and gently guide the quantum jump. The coming fifty years should be dedicated to bringing together the intellectual, social, and spiritual resources of our brilliant species to lay the foundations for the next stage of human evolution. Fortunately, many such pioneering programs, online and in person, have already been established.

Online Programs and Courses

The internet appears to be cultivating the seeds of the conscious evolution educational vision. Through websites, blogs, and online teleseminars, courses, and summits, evolutionary thought leaders are exploring and teaching various aspects of conscious evolution. The Shift Network and Evolving Wisdom are two companies that have particularly capitalized on the internet's potential to bring conscious evolution into mainstream conversation.

Beyond that, individual thought leaders are creating their own platforms to create communities around their knowledge and teachings. In Terry Patten's *Beyond Awakening* teleseminar series he has interviewed many of the world's cutting-edge evolutionary thought leaders and exposed hundreds of thousands of people to their work. And some of those evolutionary leaders are teaching seminars or posting regularly on their blogs; they include major teachers such as Ken Wilber, Deepak Chopra, Ervin Laszlo, Neale Donald Walsch, Jean Houston, Ilia Delio, Hazel Henderson, Elisabet Sahtouris, and many more.

In my own work, the internet has proved vitally useful to reaching hundreds of thousands of people. On The Shift Network (www.theshiftnetwork.com), I have taught several major courses on conscious evolution, including Agents of Conscious Evolution (ACE), Metamorphosis, Guides and Mentors, Generation One, the Sacred Way of the Conscious Evolutionary, and Co-Creators Rising, several of which are digitized and available for all. We also created twenty-four hours of content that recorded what was happening around the globe for Birth 2012.

Evolutionary teachers are not yet fully coordinated, even though we are doing our best in separate locations to engender more ongoing association, shared teaching, or continuing collegiality. Although the internet helps in the connections, and conferences and occasional convenings are vital, they are not stabilized. We need more ongoing venues for the research and development of conscious evolution, such as through formal conscious evolution educational programs, some of which have been established and are described below.

FORMAL EDUCATIONAL PROGRAMS

In addition to the above-mentioned virtual educational opportunities, some in-person programs have also been created. For example, in 1999 Professor A. Harris Stone founded the Graduate Institute (www.learn.edu), based in Bethany, Connecticut, as a private, nonprofit graduate school, offering master of arts degrees in emerging and contemporary fields of study (see www.learn .edu). In 2002, the school introduced the first accredited master of arts degree program in conscious evolution, with Allan Combs, PhD, as the academic director. Professor Combs developed a transdisciplinary curriculum incorporating both social evolution and self-evolution much as they were described in the first edition of this book. To help create a field of academic study for conscious evolution, a student in the program, Sean Avila Saiter, PhD, along with Professor Combs, founded *The Journal of Conscious Evolution* (www.cejournal.org) in 2005. Currently, Professor Combs and Charles H. Silverstein, PhD, are the academic codirectors of the program. Guest faculty members over the years have included Ervin Laszlo, Duane Elgin, Peter Russell, David Peat, Elizabeth Debold, and Sally Goerner.

Another exciting new venture has emerged called Ubiquity University (www.ubiquityuniversity.org). As Paul Taylor, Ubiquity's chief marketing officer, described it to me:

> Ubiquity University aspires to be a synergy engine — a vital global learning and innovation community platform that seeks to serve as a connection ground to the millions of cutting-edge social innovators and organizations that are experimenting to co-create the new models that serve the new paradigm. As Buckminster Fuller once said, "the highest priority in education is revolution based on synergy. Thinking synergistically requires the complete reversal of our present system of the compartmentalization of knowledge." Ubiquity believes that a fusion of education and social innovation in a modular and competency-based environment, all within an evolutionary integral framework in which interior development is emphasized as much as professional competencies, represents the future of human learning and creativity.[3]

Pioneering educational efforts are arising rapidly now. For example, Wisdom University was founded by Jim Garrison to offer wisdom teachings with an evolutionary context. The university established the first Chair in Conscious Evolution, which I initiated there. Ervin Laszlo has founded the Laszlo New-Paradigm Leadership Center at the Villaggio Globale in Bagni di Lucca, Italy, which is dedicated to research and development of the paradigm in science, medicine, and education. Resonance Academy (http://academy.resonance.is) communicates and teaches the work of world-renowned physicist Nassim Haramein, and the building of a learning community by Teresa Collins. John F. Kennedy University (www.jfku.edu) and the California Institute of Integral Studies (www.ciis.edu) are already-well-established educational institutions with an evolutionary perspective. The University of Santa Monica (www.universityofsantamonica.edu), founded by H. Ronald Hulnick and Mary Hulnick, offers experiential education for self- and social evolution. All these initiatives and more are helping to develop the field of conscious evolution.

Yet the evolutionary movement is still outside the mainstream of the academic world. Most universities do not teach conscious evolution. They lack the context, the perspective, and the whole-systems approach. We need to bring this powerful, vital worldview into the mainstream of the educational world to reach the brilliant young minds in universities, and at all levels of education, who have to take on the heavy load of dealing with the crises and potentials facing the coming generation.

Once we do, education for conscious evolution will attract innovators in every field. Students will study the world as a whole system in transition from one phase of evolution to the next — identifying breakdowns and viewing problems as evolutionary drivers leading to innovation and transformation. Through their studies, the students will discover their evolutionary vocations and connect to people and projects that need their skills. We find out what we are really capable of in the context of the evolution of our species as a whole.

A Master's Program in Conscious Evolution

What follows is a template for graduate study in the field of conscious evolution. The program can serve as a catalyst to launch the new metadiscipline of conscious evolution, designed for those who choose to be leaders of positive change in this century. It

A Master's Program in Conscious Evolution

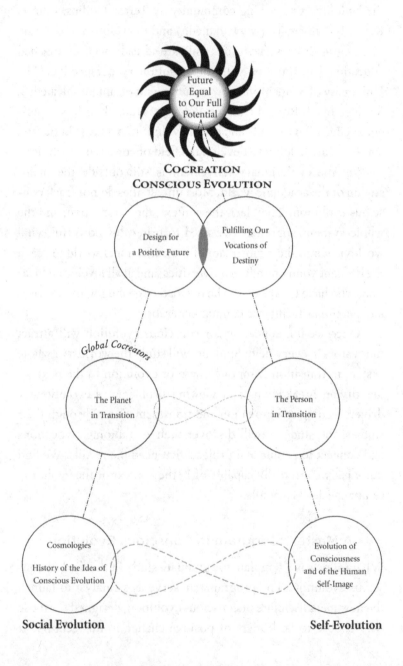

Future
Equal
to Our Full
Potential

Cocreation
Conscious Evolution

Design for
a Positive Future

Fulfilling Our
Vocations of
Destiny

Global Cocreators

The Planet
in Transition

The Person
in Transition

Cosmologies

History of the Idea of
Conscious Evolution

Evolution of
Consciousness
and of the Human
Self-Image

Social Evolution

Self-Evolution

focuses on the processes for evolutionary action, action that emerges from this worldview and how we can contribute to it. Participants will bring a high level of mastery from many fields, accompanied by a deep calling to leverage their skills in vocations of social innovation and planetary change.

Education in conscious evolution builds upon students' knowledge and skill and their desire to enhance their vocational fields. For example, the same way a computer scientist at IBM might get a master's in business administration, professionals may choose a master's in conscious evolution to expand their understanding of how to manage their most valuable asset, themselves, thus gaining a broad, systemic understanding of where society is creating new opportunities for success.

The educational program has two concurrent themes: social evolution and self-evolution. Each theme is seen from its past, present, and future perspectives. These themes unfold concurrently, as represented in the diagram. They join at the apex of the triangle where social evolution and self-evolution converge in the work of building a cocreative society.

Education for conscious evolution is an essential component for moving toward actualizing our social potential. What is being proposed here is a coherent set of courses for a curriculum, each of which is possible, plausible, and mutually reinforcing.

The First Track

Social Evolution — Cosmogenesis

We begin by studying the past. In social evolution it is cosmogenesis — the history of the evolution of the universe from the big bang to us and beyond. We see the process as a continuous creation leading to us as cocreators. We learn from the laws and processes of evolution how to now guide evolution wisely. We study the work of such pioneers as Teilhard de Chardin, Sri Aurobindo,

Ervin Laszlo, Beatrice Bruteau, Ilia Delio, Brian Swimme, Hazel Henderson, Jean Houston, Jonas Salk, Abraham H. Maslow, Buckminster Fuller, Duane Elgin, Elisabet Sahtouris, Peter Russell, Eric Chaisson, Riane Eisler, Ken Wilber, Steve McIntosh, Ted Chu, and many other evolutionary thinkers and activists.

We consciously place ourselves in the new story as we conceive and choose our emerging future on the current turn on the Spiral. We review the disciplines — geology, biology, anthropology, history, religion, science, psychology, art, current events, and future studies — as the unfolding process of creation in all its aspects: geogenesis, biogenesis, anthropogenesis, and more. By understanding evolution as the expression of universal intelligence, now becoming conscious of itself within us, and as us, we seek to overcome the dichotomy between current evolutionists who see no design in evolution, and creationists who often propose an anthropomorphic God as creator.

The History of Conscious Evolution

Along with our study of cosmogenesis, we explore the history of the idea of conscious evolution. Transformationally motivated people are the growing edge of a great continuity of souls reaching back to the very earliest times. Evolutionaries must never think of themselves as alternative, far out, or disconnected. We are in fact the growing tip of the greatest tradition of both nature and history. We are the *new* mainstream of evolution itself. Remember, the nature of nature is to transform. Those who tend toward transformation are nature personified. And in human history there has been a continuous and growing impulse toward the regeneration and transformation of humanity.

Professor Michael Grosso traced the faith that the deep and radical regeneration of human society is possible. Identifying the idea through Western history, he wrote in *The Millennium Myth: Love and Death at the End of Time*:

It starts with the Babylonian Creation stories, the Hebrew prophets, Jesus, Paul, Joachim of Fiore, the Renaissance, the Enlightenment, the American Revolution, Boston Transcendentalism, through current visions of the end of this phase of evolution and the beginning of the next, springing from science fiction, New Age, general evolution theories, and technological innovators [all seeking to participate consciously in the transformation of *Homo sapiens*, its metamorphosis into a species capable of life ever-evolving].

This core image is revealed in John's vision of a new heaven and a new earth, and in the closely related ideas that at the end of time the very laws of nature will undergo a vast overhauling in which it may even be possible to defeat death and once and for all liberate human society from injustice, from pain, and above all, from the curse of lovelessness.... *The Millennium Myth* taps into the totally unpredictable, creative rage of the human heart and imagination.[4]

The prophecies of end times of destruction of the old world order are intuitions and premonitions of the radical discontinuity from one stage of evolution to the next — which is happening now.

We are the latest expression of what may be the most fundamental impulse of human consciousness, which separates us from the animal world. Sometimes I look at my beautiful cat, Jack. He purrs, he sleeps, he eats, he hunts, he enjoys himself, but he doesn't try to be more than a cat or even a better cat. His cathood is established. But our humanhood is still incomplete. Conscious evolution embodies the great tradition of nature and of human aspiration. It is only now, however, that it has burst upon the scene as central to our survival.

Self-Evolution — The Evolution of Consciousness

This course, which also studies the past, focuses on the origin and evolution of consciousness itself, from the first cell to us and beyond. The work of Richard Maurice Bucke, MD, in *Cosmic Consciousness* sets the stage for this study. He defined three forms of consciousness:

> (1) Simple Consciousness, which is possessed by the upper half of the animal kingdom... (2) Self Consciousness, by virtue of which man becomes conscious of himself as a distinct entity apart from the rest of the universe... (3) Cosmic Consciousness, a third form which is as far above Self Consciousness as is that above Simple Consciousness. The prime characteristic of Cosmic Consciousness is, as its name implies, a consciousness of the cosmos, that is the life and order of the universe — an intellectual enlightenment or illumination, which alone would place the individual on a new plane of existence. To this is added a state of moral exaltation, an indescribable feeling of elevation, elation, and joyousness, and a quickening of the moral sense, which is more important both to the individual and to the race than is the enhanced intellectual power. With these come what may be called a sense of immortality, a consciousness of eternal life, not a conviction that we shall have this, but the consciousness that we have it already.[5]

Bucke said that although cosmic consciousness was rare, it is now arising in many people through the natural tendency of evolution to create higher consciousness. Our goal is the stabilization of ourselves at the new norm. Students would experience the broadest variety of teachers and teaching to support them in moving toward this goal.

The Evolution of Our Self-Image

In this course we also reflect upon the evolution of self-image throughout history. Our self-image deeply affects our behavior. O. W. Markley wrote in "Human Consciousness in Transformation":

> A variety of writing throughout history indicates that the underlying images held by a culture or a person have an enormous influence on the fate of the holder. No one knows the total potentiality of humankind, and our awareness of human "nature" is selective, shaped by our explicit and implicit images. In a provocative book, *The Image of the Future*, the Dutch sociologist Fred Polak noted that when the dominant images of a culture are anticipatory, they "lead" social development and provide direction for social change. They have, as it were, a "magnetic pull" toward the future, by their attractiveness and legitimacy they reinforce each movement that takes society toward them, and they influence the social decisions that will bring them to realization. As a culture moves toward the achievement of goals inherent in its dominant images, the implications of the images are explored, progress is made, and needs are more fully satisfied.[6]

In this program we study the self-images humans have held in India, Greece, China, Israel, Christendom, the Renaissance, and the modern, existentialist, and postmodern eras to discover the effects of various self-images on human behavior and well-being. For example, imagine the different effects of the following beliefs:

- This life is merely a test for the next life.
- Whatever condition you are in, it is your fate or karma from past lives and there is nothing you can do to change it.

- There is no meaning to the universe, and your life is of no significance except what you give it.
- Everything you do counts forever. You are an expression of the whole process of creation; you are a cocreator.

What do we really want to be when we grow up? As memes or idea systems can be chosen for society, so too can our self-images be selected through intuition and alignment with our soul's purpose. The process of choosing a self-image can be guided only by accessing that soul purpose, that deeper calling, and surrendering to it. As we see ourselves, so we become. Students are charged with consciously creating self-images — higher-self portraits. Noetic technologies — the science of intellect — including the implicate processes of the mind such as intuition, reframing, and visioning are used.

THE SECOND TRACK

Social Evolution — The Planet in Transition

In the second track we study the present. In social evolution it is the study of our planet in transition. We have already seen the present as a period of our birth with all systems in transition. We have imagined fully functioning innovation websites and platforms. Our breakthroughs and innovations are connected. Our successes are communicated as the NewNews through many outlets. The networks are networking. Innovators from every field often seen on the NewNews and other such media are becoming familiar newsmakers. All these activities are the living school of conscious evolution.

Students reconceptualize the planet as a whole system in transition from one phase of evolution to the next, recognizing our problems as evolutionary drivers and our breakthroughs as connected points of transformation that reveal the emerging civilization. These breakthroughs are the work of social innovators in all fields. They form the heart and soul of the curriculum for conscious evolution. Their way of living and their work, books, recordings, podcasts, and projects are the basis of study. This ever-expanding group is on the internet, increasing the synergy and interaction at the growing edge of positive change.

Students are invited to study the breakdown/breakthrough model of whole-system transformation. They identify leading organizations that are mapping the suffering and destruction, such as the World Watch Institute, the World Wildlife Fund, the Sierra Club, the Natural Resources Defense Council, Amnesty International, Human Rights Watch, and Direct Relief International, to fully understand the nature of the problems we face. Then they seek out the points of transformation — the social innovations and solutions that are cropping up everywhere in relation to the problems. They study the work and the people who are changing the world and solving real-world problems. Whenever possible, leaders of positive change become mentors. As students become engaged in the mapping and mentoring process, their evolutionary vocations are stirred and it becomes easier for them to see what they really want to do in the world. (I can hardly imagine what this would have meant to me when I was a college student. It would have saved me at least twenty years.)

Self-Evolution — The Person in Transition

As with the social evolution course described above, this second course on self-evolution studies the present. In it we study the person in transition. We apply the breakdown/breakthrough model to ourselves. We are each cells in the living body of the larger whole. Whatever is happening to us is both personal and part of the whole, just as every cell in our biological body is both unique and part of the body. Whatever we are going through is part of the planetary struggle to evolve. Our personal crises are also integral efforts to evolve ourselves as members of the larger body. We do not do this work for ourselves alone.

In this course we ask ourselves, "What in our lives is not working? What do we need to heal, mature, evolve? And what *is* working — what is breaking through? What are our peak experiences, our high-performance capacities?" With this model we begin to design our self-development programs. Our spirituality, our creativity, our relationships and vocations are nurtured and encouraged. Evolutionary circles are formed to provide an environment of spiritual intimacy, nonjudgment, and safety to bring forth our full potential. Faculty guide and coach us to refine our programs. Then we commit to the practices required to achieve higher states of being. The evolutions of society and self are inextricably interrelated and interdependent. Just as we encourage the social innovations that can bring society as a whole to a higher quality for all, so we encourage personal practices and principles of cocreation to evolve the individual, such as acceptance, affirmative prayer, community building, healing, nonviolence, synergy, meditation, networking, visioning. We are entering upon a lifelong path: the path of the cocreator, both social and personal.

Students are offered the best of modern teachers in every area: spiritual growth, creativity, relationship, health, diet, and vocation. While studying those they most admire, plus doing inner work, students begin to embody their higher-self portraits. They create vivid descriptions of themselves in a flow state, early self-images of themselves as cocreators — universal humans. As we see ourselves, so we become. Our self-image becomes the basis of our personal course of self-development.

THE THIRD TRACK

Social Evolution — The Design for a Positive Future

Now we enter the convergence process together. Students, mentors, colleagues, innovators, and friends join in an extraordinary process of cocreation. Its purpose is to initiate an ongoing process to design a world that works for everyone. This design would be drawn from the study of social innovations working in every field and sector of the wheel.

One of the world's most creative social designers, Hazel Henderson, wrote in *The Politics of the Solar Age* about the need to redesign all our systems in the coming of a new era of enlightenment: "A Solar Age is based on light-wave and solar technologies. In this Solar Age, we humans would engage in a bottom-to-top design revolution. The centralization of industrialism would give way to a new devolution: We would reshape our production, agriculture, architecture, academic disciplines, governments, and companies to align them with nature's productive processes in a new search for suitable, humane, and ecologically sustainable societies."[7]

As a complement to Henderson's focus on sustainability on Earth, Eric Drexler (one of the innovators of the radical new capacity called nanotechnology, the ability to build atom by atom, emulating nature itself) wrote in *Engines of Creation*:

> Molecular assemblers will bring a revolution without parallel since the development of ribosomes, the primitive assemblers of the cell. The resulting nanotechnology can help life spread beyond Earth — a step without parallel since life spread beyond the seas. It can help mind emerge in machines — a step without parallel since mind emerged in primates. And it can let our minds renew and remake our bodies — a step without any parallel at all. . . . These revolutions will bring dangers and opportunities too vast for the human imagination to grasp.[8]

This is the design work for the positive future. It has never been done before, and it will never be finished. Students will be helping to form the future in the present. They will not be working with blue-sky visions or dreams, but with practical capacities already existing to build our field of dreams. Mentors in each sector of social change meet with students in a prolonged "design science revolution," as called for by Buckminster Fuller, Hazel Henderson, Ervin Laszlo, and others. Working on both the internet and onsite, students and their mentors enter the ongoing process of codesigning futures based on what works.

Self-Evolution — Fulfilling Our Vocations of Destiny

Students pick areas of their choice and have opportunities to work on ideas, projects, and initiatives with people who are doing the work that excites them. This contact stimulates and deepens vocation. Through this process the participants' life purpose is enriched and fulfilled in an environment of excitement and discovery. The joy of learning is now expanded to include connecting our talents with meaningful work and wherever possible with people and projects to work with — the key to self-actualization. Remember Maslow's discovery: The key to self-actualization — a life of creativity and joy — is to find work that is intrinsically valuable and self-rewarding.

Although many current jobs are disappearing, the idea of work as creative expression is growing. In the new schools for conscious evolution, students discover the full meaning of vocational education. The education for conscious evolution elevates the concept of vocation to mean life purpose in the service of self and society. It also emphasizes social entrepreneurship as a way to actualize our own creativity with others who are attracted to the same purpose. Liberal arts are vital to help us understand and envision what we choose to create, just as all other branches of learning become essential instruments in our evolution.

Schools for conscious evolution help fulfill our great drive for self-expression — self-actualization through meaningful work and chosen life purpose. They become magnets not only for current cultural creatives, but for the far larger number of incipient evolutionaries — imaginal cells in waiting. When this field is established, it will draw to it those ready to participate in the evolution of self and society. I imagine this would be a majority of the young and many of us seeking vocations that excite us — at whatever age.

Visions of a Cocreative Society

At the apex of our program is the yet mysterious cocreative society, the next stage of human evolution. Out of education in conscious evolution there emerges an intuitive and intellectual understanding of the quantum transformation. The societal butterfly is revealed in all its glory.

Visions of our future will be developed, cultivated, dramatized, and communicated to the ever-growing community of cocreators. The magnetic field of our collective potential will draw us forward to realize it. When we build the field of our dreams, we, humanity, will come to fulfill ourselves. When there is no vision, people perish. When there is vision, people flourish.

PART IV

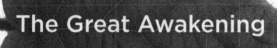

The Great Awakening

CHAPTER FIFTEEN

The Great Awakening: A Planetary Birth Experience in Our Lifetimes

The world is ready for the advent of a new stage of human consciousness and action. It is time for a "planetary birth experience," a collective awakening, an experience of shared empathy, love, and creativity. Just as we once evolved from Neanderthal to *Homo sapiens* through a mysterious set of circumstances, not fully understood, so now we are emerging as *Homo universalis*, a species capable of conscious evolution on Earth and beyond.

What are signs of the emergence of a new era of evolution? Ken Carey wrote in *The Third Millennium*:

> A mother never knows exactly what hour she will give birth to her child, but she has a "due date," an approximate time when the baby is expected and will most likely be born. For millennia now there have been those in various traditions of both East and West who have known that the earth has a due date sometime during the second decade of the 21st century. Though there will be much awakening of

individuals prior to the first unified movement of the awakened planetary organism, this movement, like a first breath,
will occur in but a single moment.[1]

Such a planetary awakening is happening now because the
timing is right in relationship to our planetary life cycle. Let's
continue with our biological analogy. A newborn baby awakens
at a specific time in its life cycle, just after it has made its journey
from the comfort of the womb into the harsh and strange world.
The child finally rests at peace. At one delightful moment, which
cannot be predicted yet is expected, the infant awakens, relaxes,
opens eyes that have never seen — eyes that were created in the
darkness of the womb. For the first time the womb-veil thins, light
floods in, and the infant focuses and sees its mother. A radiant
glow of recognition and joy crosses its face and animates its body.
It has come home to the new world, never to go back again.

Let's compare ourselves as a planetary organism to a biological organism just after birth. We are facing a trauma that could
be compared to the trauma a baby faces after birth. We are Generation One, the first generation on this Earth to consciously be
aware that we can destroy ourselves by our own actions or evolve
ourselves by our own choices. We are struggling to coordinate
ourselves as one global system, feeling the panic of running out of
Mother Earth's resources. We are learning to change our energy
consumption, to grow our food in healthier ways, to handle our
own waste, to stop overpopulating and polluting, and far more.
As we do so, we are beginning to recognize we are all members of
one planetary body.

For the first time, in the 1960s during the Apollo program we
opened our Earth-bound eyes, saw ourselves from outer space,
and were amazed at the beauty of our Earth as a whole. For one
brief moment we saw no boundaries, no nations, and no walls to
divide us.

Now, millions of us are awakening to our participation in the whole, as our planetary body integrates and links up throughout the world. The internet, mobile phones, social media, and many other elements of our rapidly growing planetary nervous system are connecting us as individuals and groups, beyond the confines of time and space.

The process is unfolding. Let's imagine that the internet is informing us of what is now working to evolve our world. Let's assume that the NewNews in all its forms is communicating to us the news of who we are becoming. But we are still in a post-natal torpor, traumatized and confused by the abruptness of the changes we are undergoing. Many of us are without hope, without the sense that our future is desirable and attractive, forgetting that each of us has a part to play. Yet, as Teilhard de Chardin writes in *The Future of Man*, "The whole future of the Earth, as of religion, seems to me to depend on the awakening of our faith in the future."[2] At times, we live with an ominous sense of impending doom, which is realistic. We have never seen another planet go through a transition period wherein its inhabitants were able to create so many offspring, so much technology, and such high levels of pollution and waste. If we do not quickly adjust to our new condition, we may die. Our birth could be a death. The dangers we face are life threatening, just as the newborn infant faces critical problems that must be quickly handled or it will die.

Something more is needed to awaken us as a whole — an infusion of life, love, appreciation, and security to comfort us in our time of trial. Remember, everything that rises converges. The planetary dissipative structure is reaching maximum instability. Everything we do counts, especially in this critical time. Will the impulses of health and creativity prevail soon enough to counter the acceleration toward environmental and social breakdown?

A Planetary Birth: A Life-Changing Experience

Among the many things that are needed to facilitate the positive shift is a catalytic series of events to connect us spiritually, emotionally, and practically — events with such powerful impacts that the global state of mind will be changed, events so inspiring that the world will never again doubt that we have the capacity and the will to make it, that everyone on Earth has a chance to survive and grow, that each of us is needed, and that all of us are part of the universal creative process.

Originally, I envisioned a single Planetary Birth Day celebration. We had had two great Earth Days to awaken us to our environmental crisis. This, however, was to be the first Planetary Birth Day. It would awaken us to our creativity, our love, and our potential for life ever evolving.

The vision for this Planetary Birth Day first came to me on an afternoon walk in Connecticut in February of 1966. The trees stood black and brittle against the winter sky. I wrapped my scarf around my face and set out walking. I had been reading Reinhold Niebuhr on the subject of community, and he quoted St. Paul's famous statement: "For as the body is one, and hath many members, and all the members of that one body, being many are one body, so also is Christ."

I started contemplating what story we had that was equivalent to the birth of Christ — what story would change everything? My thoughts quieted. I was poised from within to catch the slightest hint of revelation. Suddenly, my mind's eye penetrated beyond the blue cocoon of Earth, lifting me up into the utter blackness of outer space. From there I witnessed the entire sweep of Earth's history, as though I were seeing a Technicolor movie.

I saw Earth as a living body, just as the astronauts did. It was *alive.*

I experienced a kinesthetic imprint of the planetary organism.

I felt myself to be a cell in that body. Earth was gasping for breath, struggling to coordinate itself as a whole. I felt hunger, war, torture, disease, and species extinction. The pain was so great that we all literally stopped and paid attention to the suffering at the same moment. This shared pain was the trigger for the planetary birth experience.

Then I witnessed a flash of light, more radiant than the sun, surround the planet. Empathy began to course through our planetary body and through all people. The walls that separated us spiritually dissolved. Each of us began to hear in our own inner voices and see in our own images the experience of Spirit. I felt the various organs in the social body — innovations in health, education, energy, justice, and spirituality — begin to coordinate into a whole system. I felt an uprising of light. We were becoming a glowing Earth. I heard a tone, a vibration of resonance, connecting all of us in a moment of global coherence.

Then I heard these inner words clearly: "Our story is a birth. It is the birth of humankind as one body. What Christ and all great beings came to Earth to reveal is true. We *are* one body, born into this universe. *Go tell the story of our birth.*"

I saw billions of us open our collective eyes and smile. It was a planetary smile, like the first smile of a newborn baby: When seeing her mother, her tiny face relaxes into an amazing radiant smile. She knows her mother, even though she has never seen a human being. Just so, each of us has a deep place within our heart that experiences some aspect of the Light of Life itself.

This expanded vision deeply imprinted itself in my consciousness. Every time I shared the experience, it was almost like "remembering" something that had actually happened to me personally. Since I had intuited a new vocation — as a storyteller of the birth experience to help others feel it — I was always looking for opportunities to manifest the vision in real terms. I made a beautiful film called *Visions of a Universal Humanity*, which describes the actual planetary birth experience and calls us all to manifest it in action. Visit Evolve.org to rent the film on demand or buy the DVD.

Elements of the Great Awakening

When I first wrote this book in 1998, I envisioned an event something like the first Earth Day for our Birth Day, in the model of the great Live Aid global satellite broadcast in 1985, which linked more than two billion people for eighteen hours on the theme of hunger. Our Planetary Birth Day would link as many, if not more, for a twenty-four-hour celebration of the creative potential of humanity in the third millennium.

As I developed the idea, I asked myself, What elements would be key to such an event? What ingredients could contribute to our ongoing planetary birth experience?

The first element is spiritual. Everyone who prays, meditates, or contemplates does so during such events. We have prepared for this element during many world healing and world peace days. Countless people are already linking up in meditations across the planet. For events related to our planetary birth experience, everyone is asked to participate at the same time. This is possible in today's globally connected world. During these kinds of experiences, people from every religion, culture, and tradition are aligning their thoughts and prayers on humanity's potential for goodness and creativity.

Prayers and meditations are communicated via all media from all regions of the world. Poems of praise for the potential of humanity are heard around the world. Forgiveness is offered and received as groups everywhere pray that the illusion of separation be dissolved and ask for forgiveness for the pain we have inflicted upon one another, upon other species, and upon Earth herself.

The second element is emotional; it touches the heart. Musicians perform live in all parts of the world, playing their indigenous music in celebration of humanity's potential. The music arouses our love and compassion. We feel empathy toward one another, expanding beyond family, tribe, and nation to embrace the world. We feel the excitement and expansion that often bursts forth in large parades and celebrations and during great sports events.

Imagine planetary concerts. All kinds of music interweave until we hear one planetary beat, one musical heartbeat pulsating rhythmically throughout Earth. It entrances and aligns our hearts and minds. One sound that can be hummed and sung in every tongue emerges from the planetary symphony. It is said that the note may be D-flat, known as the tone of Earth. It is the vibration that has been measured coming forth from healers in the act of healing. People attune to the tone. Brain waves and heartbeats synchronize. Tensions ease, intuitions rise, and love is felt as a palpable opening of the heart.

A third great element is the practical. From every region and culture social innovators and creators link up via the internet and phones, communicating the NewNews from all over the world, as imagined by Neale Donald Walsch in his biography of me entitled *The Mother of Invention*.[3] Pragmatic and caring voices say to the planetary child, "We can feed, we can house, we can educate, we can restore, we can explore, we can cooperate, we can cocreate." For we are already doing it when we are in coherence, resonance, and connection with what's working. Vignettes of successful projects are communicated via global satellite, just as instances of overcoming hunger were communicated during Live Aid, interspersed at that time with the song "We Are the World." The combination of prayers, music, and demonstrations causes a new awareness to course through the minds of billions of people simultaneously. Such events reveal the trends that these innovations can lead to, inviting artists, poets, and dancers to celebrate their visions of what humanity can become when we grow up.

Let your imagination soar now and see that people begin to gather in the streets, malls, churches, temples, mosques, in the bush and fields, in cities, towns, and villages. When the Berlin Wall came down people joined in joyful celebration of their liberation. Now thousands of Berlin Walls begin to come down — the walls within our hearts that hold back the pent-up love dammed by our illusion of separation and our fear of one another. Not only do we remember that Earth has no physical boundaries or borders, but we now feel in our hearts that false stereotypes, labels, and customs do not divide us against one another. We feel an uprising of love and forgiveness.

We have had many intimations of this type of experience: We felt it during VJ Day when the war with Japan was over. I was in an apartment in New York City when the announcement came. I heard a roar from the city as people opened their windows and cried out with joy. People flooded into the streets. An irresistible tide of relief and celebration brought people into each other's arms. Strangers were hugging and kissing with abandon. I went into the street and was carried away by the enthusiasm of the crowd.

We felt it again when Neil Armstrong set foot on the moon. Bells rang throughout the world. We identified ourselves as the people of Earth on a new world. We saw glimpses of such outpouring in the "Reach Out and Touch" ceremonies at the 1984 Olympics, when people in the stadium were asked to reach out and touch people from all nations and backgrounds. As I watched the feelings mount, I knew that a sense of joining wanted to spill out of the stadium, that the millions watching on television wanted to reach out also. But we were isolated in our separate homes.

It happened again during Live Aid. It happens during worldwide meditations; it happens whenever two or more of us are joined together in our love for Earth, for one another, and for Spirit. Now it's beginning to happen more consciously, in real time, to celebrate and affirm what is being born now.

Birth 2012

On December 22, 2012, fourteen years after this book was first published in 1998, I coproduced (with Stephen Dinan, CEO at The Shift Network) an actual live planetary birth experience called Birth 2012. December 21, 2012, marked the end of a phase of the Mayan calendar, and many people mistakenly interpreted that event as marking the "end of the world." Mass media told stories of apocalypse; people were selling their homes and running away to hide. It was obvious to most of us that the world was not going to end on that day. But it was true that *something* was ending: the form of consciousness marked by the illusion that we are separate from nature, from Spirit, and from one another.

In response to this transition, my Foundation for Conscious Evolution came together with Dinan's Shift Network — a teleseminar company that communicates the messages of hundreds of transformational, spiritual, and evolutionary teachers — to cocreate a global event called Birth 2012 to celebrate the birth of a new era of evolution. A remarkable gathering of people at hubs, in circles, and at celebrations occurred all over the world.

We had 537 registered hubs in countries including Australia, Brazil, Canada, Egypt, England, Scotland, Guatemala, Mexico, India, Thailand, Japan, Kenya, and the United States. The event was broadcast on PeaceDay TV online through several hundred sites. A portion was broadcast on Peace of Mind TV, which may have reached as many as ten million viewers on TV and the web in India.

All of us who participated experienced a sense of awakening to immeasurable potential. Dinan had set up a broadcasting studio at the Agape International Spiritual Center in Culver City, California. Reports were coming in live from around the world. For example, one event, in Boulder, Colorado, assembled hundreds of people for a daylong festival of cocreation, celebration, dancing, good food, and connecting. There was also a vibrant show on the Agape stage, with dancing and musical presentations. A highlight for me was when Sister Judy Cauley of the Sisters of St. Joseph arose and read with a passionate heart this new prayer, which was written for the occasion:

PRAYER TO CELEBRATE OUR PLANETARY PENTECOST
Spirit of the living God,
life of all life,
light of all light,
fertile Dark Mystery,
God-Becoming in the sacred adventure of evolution,
we are grateful to be your chosen ones,
planetary pilgrims,
cocreators with you on the edge of evolution.

This is our moment.
We are the ones
flaring forth as a flame of love
in Holy Communion with all creatures, continents,
planets, galaxies in time and space.

Great Mystery, One Spirit,
Birther of the Cosmos,
God in evolution,
We place our faith and trust in you
birthing within creation
a Planetary Pentecost.

May this be the ground from which
all our acts of love grow.

Amen. Amen. Amen.

Dinan and I had invited an illustrious group of colleagues to serve as the "Welcoming Committee" throughout the whole year of 2012. Their role was to welcome in the new era of our conscious evolution. Together they represented hundreds of thousands, if not millions, of people whose lives were touched by their work, and by the Birth 2012 celebration. Several of them were there that evening, including Rev. Michael Bernard Beckwith, Jack Canfield, James O'Dea, and Neale Donald Walsch. For various reasons the many women on the Welcoming Committee could not come. I stood there on the Agape stage surrounded by these loving men, as though they were holding the bassinet for the newborn planetary child.

Each member of the Welcoming Committee wrote an excellent essay for the book I was putting together called *Birth 2012 and Beyond: Humanity's Great Shift to the Age of Conscious Evolution*. The very titles of their essays tell the new story:

Rev. Michael Bernard Beckwith: "The Birth of a Global Citizenry"

Rinaldo Brutoco: "Ascent of the Phoenix: Global Reconstruction"

Jack Canfield: "Self-Actualization, Life Purpose, and the Evolutionary Shift"

Ashok K. Gangadean: "Dear Planetary Family"

Jean Houston: "Living on the Eve of the New Story"

Ervin Laszlo: "Global Bifurcation: The 2012 Decision Window"

Dot Maver: "Coming Together to Coauthor a New Story"

Lynne McTaggart: "Our New Story: Recognizing the Bond"
Oscar Miro-Quesada: "A Shamanic Re-Membering of Universal Humanity"
James O'Dea: "The Birth of the Peace Child"
Lynne Twist: "The Ancient Prophecy of the Eagle and the Condor"
Neale Donald Walsch: "The Overhaul of Humanity"

These thinkers and their insights represent the new mainstream, setting a new norm of the shared vision of our future. Together their networks reach millions of people.

The Legacy of Birth 2012

After Birth 2012, I felt depressed, not unlike a mother experiencing postpartum depression after a child is born. I couldn't find the baby. What really had happened?

Then I realized that that first celebration had merely been an *announcement* of the birth. It was like the story told of Jesus' birth in a manger. Only the wise ones knew that something new had happened. Yet it really had happened.

Something new has happened *within* us. We are the baby! A new consciousness, a new love, a greater awareness of pain throughout the whole is manifesting. I felt it within myself, as did many others, as though I were shifting from a self-conscious, separated human to a "universal" human, connected through the heart to the whole of life and awakened from within to a deeper soul's purpose, aware of higher frequencies of Spirit within myself incarnating the greater light.

Although Birth 2012 was a vital contribution to our birthing process, I no longer sense that the birth will happen in a single moment, on that long-awaited "due date." It's a process. An accumulative series of experiences is birthing this new stage of our evolution — in-person as well as virtual gatherings, on the individual, local, and global scale. Many hubs, circles, and gatherings formed to celebrate Birth 2012, and they are continuing and spreading. One valuable revelation that came from Birth 2012 is that we really can create global events celebrating the next era of evolution. The time is right: the media are available, our planetary nervous system is ready to link up, the internet is already connecting the new capacities of the social body, our prayers are aligning our thoughts, and the music is opening our hearts.

I sense that our planetary birth experience is happening across time and space now in a series of events great and small as we allow the love we feel for one another, for nature, and for Spirit to overtake us and unite us. As we place our conscious attention on doing this, I sense we are just beginning to open our eyes together. I sense that a joy and newness of hope are coursing through those of us who are participating.

Many of us sense that we are a united humanity awakening to the fact that we have always been one planetary body. We are beginning to open our eyes together and see the light of who we are becoming — all parts of one global family with the capacity to care for all its members. We are ready to discover the vast and unknown potential of an awakened humanity in a universe of immeasurable dimensions and life-forms.

The Process of Cocreation Continues

We can imagine that social innovators will continue coming together in processes of cocreation. New social architecture for cocreation is becoming visible, such as the Wheel of Cocreation, which I and many others have used in our work, and which I describe in detail in chapter 11. We are discovering ways of experiencing both the alignment of loving consciousness and the increased interaction among innovating elements, all of which can be communicated worldwide. I feel strongly that the patterns connecting us will continue to be strengthened, and that millions more are being aroused to join in the effort to grow and nurture a new world.

Let's dedicate the third millennium to the evolution of our species. Let's each declare that we are to become a universal humanity, coevolutionary with nature and cocreative with Spirit. We are at a new beginning. The great awakening is happening. The twenty-first century is in full stride. We can move through the crisis of our birth without devastating all life on Earth. Let's continue creating events and celebrations that help usher in this new era.

CHAPTER SIXTEEN

The Cocreative Society Revealed

The cocreative society has been imagined by seers of all cultures, envisioned as heaven on Earth, the new Jerusalem, Paradise, the Promised Land. In some deep sense we all know it, and long for it, for it has been told to us since time immemorial. It is ourselves fulfilled. Now we see that this new state of being is not life after death, but life at the next turn of the Evolutionary Spiral.

Reviewing Our New Story

To envision the cocreative society, we review our new story — the story of the emergence of universal humanity and of the individual cocreator maturing in the fullness of time, when the noosphere is ripening, when we have increasing abundance, access to knowledge, personal freedom, and an unprecedented ability to choose our own destinies.

The cocreative society occurs when this superorganism, this noosphere, this immense collective power of modern society is consciously and lovingly oriented toward the evolution of humanity. It is the result of our awakening to our capacity to restore Earth, to free ourselves from poverty and disease, to further emancipate individual creativity, to develop synergistic social and economic systems, and to convert our military-industrial-technological complex to the restoration, protection, and enhancement of life on Earth, and the exploration and development of outer space and universal life.

The cocreative society cannot be imposed or engineered into existence. It is nurtured into being by increasing the connections and coherence among those already initiating vital actions. It emerges when we collectively overcome the illusion of separation that has divided us, for the capacities we need — the technology, resources, and know-how — are already present in their early stages to realize our evolutionary agenda. A catalytic spark of shared love and spiritual experience combined with the evolutionary drivers we face is needed to activate the great genius of humanity to join in inspired actions. The great awakening is a vision of such a catalytic event.

The cocreative society may seem impossibly difficult from the historical perspective, but from the evolutionary perspective we are encouraged. For 13.8 billion years, including five mass extinctions, life has been increasing in consciousness, freedom, and complex order. Now place ourselves in that continuum. Imagine us as early humans, shivering in caves with nothing to protect us from the weather, starvation, and animals far stronger and quicker, being told that one day we would have to protect other species and care for nature herself. Imagine yourself as a pioneer seeing for the first time the Pacific Ocean and being asked to envision today's Los Angeles. Since all that happened, we cannot doubt that the next step is possible, and indeed, inherent in the nature of reality.

A Preview of Coming Attractions

In our movie of creation, we allow ourselves to see ahead and to feel what it is like to be at the next stage of our evolution. Let us now stand together in the future-present and welcome ourselves. Let's take the quantum jump and preview the coming attractions.

Our purpose here is to use our intuition and see our future based on potentials now awakening within us, so that we can propel ourselves forward to fulfill our destiny. Our intuition is not based on mere dreaming, but rather on our deepest intentions, choices, and capacities, both known and emerging. We are going forward now to imagine what it will be like when everything we know we can do works.

To cocreate this image of a positive future, we connect peaks of human performance and exceptional ability, from mountaintop to mountaintop. Let's draw an imaginary line from peak to peak and establish a new plateau of excellence and creativity based on the best we can do in all fields. Let's awaken our memory of the future and feel what it is like when we are whole, healthy, and normal beyond the illusion of our separation. When there is no vision people perish, but when there *is* vision, we flourish, grow, emancipate, and create that which we desire.

This vision of the future is my intuition and heart's desire. It is what I choose. It is what I stand for. As you read, consider your choices, your deepest longing for a future, not in the immediate moment, but perhaps five hundred years hence, when we are in the next stage of evolution. What do you see when you imagine our highest creativity connected and established as a new normalcy?

What It May Be Like as We Evolve

Let's lift ourselves for a moment beyond the blue cocoon of Earth. Penetrating the vastness of the universe, floating in weightlessness as our astronauts do, we see a few frames ahead in our movie of creation. We are becoming fully human. Our cosmic consciousness is stabilized. We experience infinitely expanding awareness, deeper and deeper interrelatedness. The veil of matter has disappeared. Reality is more like a thought than a thing. Empathy increases and intentionally expands.

We make direct contact with the evolving core of the Spiral — with universal intelligence. The designing process that is forever creating the universe breaks into our awareness as our own motivation, as we begin to cocreate on a planetary scale. As mentioned previously, centuries ago great religious avatars came to this planet in a state of cosmic consciousness — the Indian seers, Akhenaton, Moses, Buddha, Jesus, and Mohammed. They sensed themselves as directly connected with Source. All taught an ethic of love, a faith in the process of creation, and a promise of life beyond the body of the individual and the planet.

Few ordinary people could share their experience, so religions, dogmas, and institutions formed to hold the promise. Now, because of the natural rise of consciousness and freedom, millions are experiencing direct personal contact with a deeper reality. Spiritual connection with Source, or the metapattern, becomes the norm and is stabilized because a critical mass has achieved it. Mass resonance reinforces it, and the nervous system of the social body, our mass media, is communicating stories of people who are in that state as the norm. Every day we hear what we can do that is good. We begin now to catch a glimpse of the glory of our full potential self — universal humanity growing up.

We gain continuity of consciousness with all dimensions of reality in an eternal present, a nonlocal field of all possibilities out of which everything is always evolving, as the great avatars have always demonstrated. Our awareness incorporates both the eternal and the evolving aspect of God. We are able to maintain our eternal oneness — the still center — while manifesting, as the creative intelligence does, in space and time.

The genius that built us from a fertilized egg to a human being is our genius. We are that which we know. We gain knowledge by identity. We are the creative genius of our own body-minds. The secrets of the atomic, molecular, and cellular worlds are revealed to us when we are at one with the process of creation through internal awareness as well as through scientific investigation. Conscious evolution ultimately means that the cosmic intelligence that is manifest in every particle and entity in the universe becomes self-aware in us, as us. The separation of the rational mind from the great creative process dissolves, and we recognize that intelligence as our own. With that intelligence, we create as we think. Descartes' dictum "I think therefore I am" becomes "I think therefore it is." Our thoughts are translated ever more directly into manifestation.

We have shifted from what Gary Zukav called in *The Seat of the Soul* the five-sensory human to the multisensory human.[1] We are naturally aware of multiple dimensions of reality. Our isolation from the spiritual world, or other dimensions, is overcome through our expanded knowing of the full spectrum of reality.

We discover there is a library of consciousness recorded in a great memory bank of what Ervin Laszlo called the "vacuum-based holofield" and the "cosmic Internet" in his book *The Whispering Pond*.[2] He hypothesized that there may be a physical medium, the vacuum-based holofield, that is self-remembering and is able to hand down the characteristics of the parent universe (universes that came before ours) to our offspring universe. That is how the great yogis can see past lives. It is all there. Nothing is lost, not a hair, not a feather. While the physical universe may be increasing in disorder, the intelligence of the universe is increasing in order and coherence. Everything is recorded in the "mind of the cosmos," is remembered, and is ultimately available to those in expanded awareness. Everything we do, experience, and think remains available. We discover that the universe is increasing in creativity, intelligence, and coherence, as are we. We realize that the direction of evolution is for the universe with its billions and billions of galaxies to become conscious of itself as a whole. This is the fulfilled vision that Eric Chaisson foresaw in *The Life Era*.

We cultivate higher states of being, here and now. Out-of-body experiences, telepathy, clairvoyance, psychokinesis — all the dormant extended capacities that were embodied in the great yogis, avatars, and founders of world religions become a new norm. We can do the work that Jesus and others did, and even greater works, for we are now born into the superorganism. We find that our metanormal capacities, as Michael Murphy said in *The Future of the Body*, are normal for universal humans.[3] We are democratizing the miraculous as the next stage of our evolution. Our higher spiritual and personal capacities, now combined and integrated with the electronic and extended capacities of the social and technological body, are a quantum jump as great as from the earliest human to us.

THE ILLUSION OF SEPARATION IS OVERCOME

As cosmic consciousness stabilizes in a critical mass, it becomes more difficult to maintain the illusion of separateness. Because millions of us are already moving in that direction and because we have imagined that we have already established a shared resonant field of this awareness through the first planetary birth experience, it is more natural for individuals to reside in the expanded state of empathy as a new norm.

The near-fatal human flaw of consciousness — the illusion that we are separate from one another, from nature, and from Spirit — is healed through the mass resonance and the emergence of millions of maturing humans who tend toward universal, holistic consciousness. Whenever this illusion is overcome, we behave lovingly to one another. In the gentle birth scenario we are calling for, the separated mind is consumed in love and an awareness of oneness. The violence that has been foreseen in Armageddon-like scenarios is avoided. A gentle planetary birth is achieved. The separated mind cannot stand apart from that field of love. When enough of us hold together, the gentle birth is facilitated.

As the illusion of separation dissolves, we see that we can coordinate ourselves naturally as one body. As love pours forth from our hearts, the larger body of universal humanity is unbounded, free at last to reveal its magnificent and beneficent collective creativity. It becomes obvious that we are all members of one body. New economic, social, educational, environmental, and political systems naturally emerge out of this consciousness. What seems (and is) impossible in self-centered consciousness is natural and normal in cosmic, whole-centered consciousness.

We Enter the Global Brain

We now have become fully connected to the global intelligence system. We are active participants in the global brain. We ask for information and receive it from the collective memory bank of the larger body, just as we now ask ourselves to find a memory and images of that experience appear on our mental screens.

Our larger global brain functions as an extended nervous system and brain for each of us. On the inner plane we are nonlocal — we are part of the one mind. On the outer plane, through our global brain, we are also nonlocal and omnipresent, accessing all information instantly, as needed.

There is a mechanical aspect to everything that has form, but our global brain is more than a machine: it is an extension of our own brain. We have integrated our extended capacities gracefully and no longer feel separated from our larger body. Future extensions of computers, phones, faxes, radios, and televisions are simply used as extensions of ourselves. As Jerome Clayton Glenn wrote in *Future Mind: Artificial Intelligence: Merging the Mystical and the Technological in the 21st Century*, "Through Conscious Technology, civilization will evolve into a continuum of technology and humanity...."[4]

WE BECOME SELF-HEALING AND SELF-REGENERATING

As we stabilize our universal consciousness and connection to Source, we become self-healing and self-regenerating beings. Our healing arts — prayer, meditation, visualization, exercise, diet, and loving care — integrate with our magnificent medical advances. We understand the language of our bodies. We resonate with and unlock the inner secrets of our body-minds.

As our consciousness grows, our bodies no longer seem like strange creatures we do not understand and bring like separate objects — a lung, a liver, a finger, a heart — to doctors to be examined under a microscope like foreign bodies. We know our bodies. We have within us what Deepak Chopra called the "great cornucopia of healing substances."[5] We become intimate with our own bodily genius and integrate the wisdom of our hearts with our intellectual understanding of how nature works. We heal and regenerate and eventually evolve our bodies by conscious choice.

We learn thereby to extend our lives by choice and to end our lives by choice. Remember, evolution raises consciousness and freedom with every turn of the Spiral. We now enter the third life cycle. The first cycle began with single cells who were semi-immortal and divided to reproduce themselves. The second cycle began with multicellular life that evolved sexual reproduction and scheduled death of the individuals, as parents learned to degenerate and die. The origin and diversity of the species began. The third cycle begins when we hit the limits to growth on the planet and begin the shift from maximum procreation to cocreation. We learn to give birth by choice, to die by choice, and to extend our lives by choice.

In the third cycle, life extension and conscious dying emerge naturally. Those who have more to create choose to live on until they are finished with their work. When we feel that our creativity has run its course, we gracefully choose to die. In fact, it seems unethical and foolish to live on. The stereotype of aging changes. People are regenerated through their creativity to live as long as the creation calls them. When we are old and tired of life and do not want to live on, we learn to die by choice, as some native people do. The sorry picture of millions of people bent with age, wishing to pass on, with nothing to do, nowhere to go, no possibility of renewal, often suffering from dementia or Alzheimer's, seems barbaric and cruel in retrospect.

It is my preference that, when I feel complete with this life, I call in my beloveds, my family, my friends. In a momentous celebration I will prepare to enter the mystery of the next phase of life and seek the blessings of those I love. I choose to make my transition gracefully.

Sexual reproduction and scheduled death evolved millions of years ago. In the third cycle they evolve once again, this time toward conscious reproduction, conscious life extension, and conscious dying. The mammalian life cycle becomes the universal life cycle. We are the generation on the cusp of this great transition. We feel it even now: increased sensitivity to the power of thought, intention, belief, and attitude in achieving optimum wellness and even rejuvenation.

We continue to transform from the current human to the cocreative human spiritually and physically as well. As Eric

Drexler said in *Engines of Creation*, quoted earlier, nanotechnology can "let our minds renew and remake our bodies."[6] When we combine our cosmic consciousness with our capacities to transform our bodies through both healing and medical advances, in an Earth-space or universal environment, we realize that the emergence of universal humanity is not a metaphor, it is a fact. As real as the evolution from *Homo neanderthal* to *Homo sapiens* is the jump from *Homo sapiens* to *Homo universalis*.

Eventually, as we learn to live beyond our planet — in the solar system and among the galaxies — we find that our bodies are not appropriate for long-distance travel. We learn to design bodies that are viable for universal life. This need may well be the long-range meaning of our new capacities such as cloning or bioengineering. Our purpose is not to redesign our bodies for life on a crowded planet, but to consciously evolve our bodies for life beyond our planet. We are crossing the great divide from creature to cocreator physically, mentally, and spiritually. Nature always creates new bodies for new frontiers; witness the sequence of bodies from fish to amphibians to mammals to humans, and now to universal humans. We are at the threshold of genuine newness. The only difference between us and other creatures who experienced a radical change is that we are entering the process consciously.

In his book *Human Purpose and Transhuman Potential: A Cosmic Vision for Our Future Evolution*, Dr. Ted Chu wrote:

> Having learned how to travel across vast space (by harvesting stars as heat engines, for example), CoBe [cosmic beings] will enter and adapt to environments totally alien to humans, and in doing so become incredibly sophisticated, converting matter and energy into what Ray Kurzweil calls "computronium." Relatively isolated CoBe

tribes may form in distant galaxies, possibly marking the beginning of a second Axial Age.[7]

From one stage of evolution, the next stage tends to look like a miracle. How would a bird look to a single cell? How does universal humanity with its godlike powers look to us? Everything is miraculous, this step no more than the rest. Why, having seen the miracle of our emergence from subatomic particles, would we be surprised at our next step of evolution?

CHOSEN CHILDREN

In the next phase of our evolution, we have chosen children. Contra-ception has become pro-ception. Parenting is a vocation, not a necessity or an accident. Not all people will choose to have children, but those who choose do it consciously and wholeheartedly. Each child is a loving act of creation. Each child is chosen, welcomed, needed, and beloved. He or she is recognized as a vital member of the social body.

Education for conscious evolution is available everywhere. It assumes the new context of universal evolution and sees the process as a continuum from the origin of creation to the present and beyond. Big History is a must for all students. The Wheel of Cocreation is not only studied but also used as a vehicle for students to seek their vocation, connect with projects that are working, and learn why and how the projects are working. They will seek out mentors and cocreators they choose to work with on their projects. Conscious evolution education is the process of discovering each child's creative expression, cultivating it as the most precious resource on Earth, and connecting it with the people and tasks where it can best flower in an ever-evolving world.

Schools open their doors — they take down their walls and release our children to become cocreators of new worlds. The needs of the world are the schools' lifelong curriculum. Everyone is a teacher to someone and everyone is a student of someone. Each child is on a quest to discover his or her purpose, gifts, and work in participation with the evolution of the larger body. Students and mentors are busy throughout the educational systems codesigning the new world, seeking the synergies among all the parts.

THE COCREATIVE COUPLE

Men and women join as coequal cocreators in the society of universal humans. The purpose of their holy union is to give birth to each other as cocreators and when ready, if so desiring, to give birth to children by choice. Each child born in the new society is welcomed as a universal human.

This shift in relationship is fundamental to planetary transformation. As women have fewer children and live longer lives, their loving creativity is rising — an irresistible tide of desire to express and find life purpose in the world. This drive is eventually as powerful as the drive to reproduce. It is the suprasexual drive to evolve ourselves. Now we become the cocreative couple, which begins when both partners achieve within themselves at least the beginning of a balance between the masculine and feminine, the animus and the anima. It begins when the woman's initiative and vocational need is received in love by the feminine receptivity of her partner. When she is loved for her more masculine side, she falls in love with the man's feminine aspect, for what she needs is the nurturance of her own strength and creativity. She loves him for his receptivity. He no longer has to prove himself by control and domination. He can bring forth his own creativity without aggression. And she can express her strength without fear of losing him. Whole being joins with whole being, recreating the family at the next stage of evolution. Same-sex couples experience a similar process of integration and joining to emancipate each other.

The breakup of the twentieth-century procreative family

structure is a vital perturbation needed for the breakthrough of the emerging cocreative family structure. The cocreative couple forms a basic unit of the cocreative society, whole beings with whole beings, neither matriarchy nor patriarchy, but partnerships, laying the foundations for the next stage of democracy, for synocracy.

SYNOCRACY EMERGES

Individualistic democracy evolves into "synocracy," or synergistic democracy. Freedom comes to mean the ability to fully express our uniqueness as vital members of the whole community. Win-lose voting develops into win-win-win decision making — how to achieve a win for both parties and for the community and environment as a whole. Because the whole is always greater than the sum of its parts, we discover that by cocreating rather than by competing, each individual and group can better achieve its fulfillment, for there is more for all. Although there is always competition to stimulate excellence, the emphasis is for each member of society to achieve his or her full potential within the whole.

Robert's Rules of Order, which was such a great advance over killing one another, becomes Synergistic Rules of Order, a win-win-win process that takes into account the interdependence of life and seeks to find a way for the self-interest of each party to be achieved by seeking common goals and matching needs and resources. The process complements rather than defeats the self-interest of others. Remember, our more unitive consciousness has been secured. We are not trying to solve our problems in the same state of consciousness in which we created them.

Government evolves from its coercive, bureaucratic phase to its new role as coordinator and facilitator of people's creativity. Genuine self-government is achieved as people become truly self-governing — that is, higher-self governing.

The vast kindergarten of humankind formerly served by the police, the welfare system, mental hospitals, and prisons gradually grows up. The problems we faced in the twentieth century are not solved; they are dissolved, as the problems of a two-year-old do not exist for a twenty-year-old.

We have no desire to overpopulate, for most people are experiencing the joys of cocreation, greater longevity, and an ever-expanding sense of participation in the whole. The military-industrial-technological complex is evolving its fundamental mission: instead of seeking the power to dominate and control for the sake of national security, it works for genuine security — the restoration of Earth and the protection of people from terrorism and planetary disasters — while it gains tremendous capacities from space exploration and development. Resources now locked in the military and in social services, which generally serve a still-immature humanity, are freed for the tasks of the evolutionary agenda. Their tasks of new world building, both on Earth and in outer space, are suitable to their highest self-images and more noble aspirations, which have been distorted by past systems of competition, and there is genuine profit to be made in environmental restoration, socially responsible business, and space development.

The hierarchy of social needs has been accepted. The vast resources and brilliance of our species are now focused on the evolutionary agenda rather than on overconsumption, excessive competition, and aggressive defense.

We still have problems, but they won't be the same ones. Our current issues of hunger, poverty, war, ignorance, greed, and injustice are all symptoms of our sense of separation from one another, from nature, and from Spirit. After we mature in our spiritual, social, and technological abilities, we find that we do know how to make the world a physical success without damage to the environment or jeopardizing anyone.

In *Abundance: The Future Is Better Than You Think*, Peter H. Diamandis and Steven Kotler document how artificial intelligence, robotics, infinite computing, nanomaterials, synthetic biology, and many other exponentially growing technologies will enable us to make greater gains in the next two decades than we have in the previous two hundred years. They write, "We will soon have the ability to meet and exceed the basic needs of every man, woman and child on the planet."[8]

The problems we will face are really unimaginable to a newly born universal humanity. Remember, we are born into a universe of billions and billions of planets, some of which may have life comparable to our own. My sense is that when we can achieve a degree of mass resonance and global coherence, we will be ready to experience other life in the universe. We have to grow up to find out, just as a newborn does.

Shared Contact to Cocreate: The Next Quantum Step in Human Evolution?

Intuition tells us that we are not alone in the universe. The time has come for people to join together in resonant groups, small and large, and simply *ask* for contact with higher intelligence: *We are a very young universal species. We have just been born into the next stage of our evolution. We do not fully know how to make this transition from the womb of Earth to existence as a cocreative species on Earth and beyond. We ask for guidance now.*

It is not a matter of the government, the media, or the defense department giving us permission. It is the right of people everywhere to seek the collective experience of positive forms of life throughout the universe. Once the experience of contact is shared by many of us, we'll realize we have entered the next phase of our evolution of universal humanity.

Our growth potential is immeasurable. We saw our faint

beginnings, for example, as we watched the *Mars Pathfinder* land on July 4, 1997. It dropped upon Mars's rocky terrain, bouncing in its balloon-like covering, until it settled and opened itself like the egg of a baby turtle. Then it deflated its covering, opened its petals, turned on its camera eyes, and prepared to crawl out! It began immediately to photograph rocks and send the pictures to Earth. It took eight minutes for the signals to go to and from Earth, so the *Pathfinder* was programmed with rules. It knew what to do when confronting a boulder or a precipice. One scientist said that the *Pathfinder* had the intelligence of a bug. He went on to say on television, "People of Earth, you are the soul of the *Pathfinder*. It is your eyes, your hands that touch the rocky soil of a new world."

And so we begin the process of bringing inanimate matter to life. Soon we learn to bring life to planets and to build little habitats in space using nonterrestrial materials and solar energy. We become an Earth/Space, or solar system, people. We are preparing for our life as a universal humanity.

Earth becomes a new world as we build new worlds in space. It is our natural and cultural home, to be loved, enhanced, and conserved in harmony with other species. The wilderness, however, is no longer on Earth; it is in the vastness of the universe, the genuine unknown. As once, long ago, life crept out of the seas onto the barren planet, we now reach beyond Mother Earth to establish our extended home beyond the biosphere, but carrying our own biosphere with us to survive. In this sense, poetically speaking, Mother Earth is giving birth to new versions of herself as the human species takes aspects of Earth and plants them in the universe beyond the womb of Earth.

Some people surmise that we are gaining these new technological capacities that seem unnatural for an Earthbound species because that is how we will give birth to galactic offspring before the sun expands and destroys all planets in the solar system, billions of years in the future. When the sun completes its life cycle and burns all its planets, we will be star children, a galactic species. Memories of our Earthbound life will be reconstructed in the way we now piece together the story of the origin of life on Earth.

Few of us can conceive of the new potentials we shall discover as we take the next step as a universal species. The benefits of exploring and developing our full range of human potential in a universal environment will lead to options inconceivable to a self-centered, Earthbound species.

We have been gestating in the womb of Earth. We may be surrounded by other life-forms, but unable to see or feel them because we have been limited in our awareness. The universe is unitary: its laws are the same throughout, its chemistry consistent. When we do meet other life, although we will be physically diverse, what we will all be increasingly conscious of is the One Source from which we all come.

On the inner plane, we emerge as beings in the image of that creative intelligence that so many call God. We are godlike in our power, we are universal, and we participate in the evolution of matter itself into conscious life. We recognize in all humility that we are an infinitesimal part of an infinite universe, capable even in our infancy of resonating with that infinity to an ever more precise degree.

A Vision of the Future:
A Fulfillment of the Aspirations of the Past

The following passage originally appeared in my book *The Evolutionary Journey*. I share it here as a vision of what is possible for us if we join together and enact the ideals presented in this book.

We are one body, all people. We coordinate as a planetary body, attuning to one another and to the designing intelligence.

We are immortal. We are not bound by the limits of the body.

We are universal. We are higher beings. Our innate sense of growth potential, our intimation of a higher state of being is true.

We are conscious cocreators, partners with God. Mystical and secular awareness unite in evolutionary consciousness as we attune to the pattern in the process and assume some responsibility for the technologies of creation.

The future affirms the past. The root of "religion" is *re-ligare*, to bind back and make whole. We are reunited with our entire evolutionary past — from our cosmic conception through our birth into the universe.

We are in contact with other life. The intimations of higher beings are affirmed. We have always been in contact intuitively. The esoteric or hidden is becoming exoteric and clear. Once we saw through a glass darkly. Now we see face to face.

We know more about the creative process. We know more of the laws of the universe as we become more creative and powerful. The laws that guide us are the laws of evolutionary process and transformation. The precedent we draw upon is 13.8 billion years of success. As infinitesimal cocreators we greet the infinite universe with the humility of hope that we are loved, we are good, we are needed, and we are capable.

The separation is over. Through expanded love and

knowledge, the desire for deeper union with the creative intelligence, God, is satisfied.

We become the second couple at the second tree — the Tree of Life. Adam and Eve were symbolically the first couple. They joined the masculine and feminine together and made a whole being, wherein they reached the Tree of the Knowledge of Good and Evil, and separated from the animal world. To reach the Tree of Life, to have access to the powers of creation, each person must become whole, uniting the masculine and feminine, the yang and the yin, the rational and the intuitive. Then we can unite whole being with whole being, cocreator with cocreator. The second couple reaches the second tree, the Tree of Life, the tree of the healing of the nations. Cosmic consciousness is secured.

We see that the meaning of our crisis is to activate our new capacities. The purpose of our new powers is universal life. Universal humanity is born, is alive, is well, and is growing. Our birth has been accomplished. We are at a new beginning.[9]

Participating in the Quantum Change

This vast vision of the next stage of our evolution may at first seem beyond us. What can anyone do as an individual, in a whole-system transformation of this order, when often it seems hard to get through the day? Our participation in the quantum change starts at home, in our personal lives, in that infinitesimal yet momentous flick of a decision to say yes to our unique potential. The quantum transformation unfolds through our joining with one another in small groups to stabilize our higher consciousness and to affirm our higher qualities of being — evolutionary circles of all kinds to birth the universal human that each of us is.

The quantum transformation continues as we discover our callings, our chosen vocations. Each life purpose is a vital element in the emerging body of humanity. As we nurture the seeds of our unique genius, we commit to growing them in the world. We form our teams and partnerships; we select initiatives to carry our life purpose into manifestation at the growing edge of change. These projects become our progeny, our offspring — they are loving expressions of our combined genius. Our commitment carries us forward to bring the inner work of personal and spiritual growth into spirit-motivated action in the world. The human potential movement grows into the social potential movement. Each of us is a seed of transformation in the social body. As we connect with one another, we design new social systems, innovations that bring forth the essential goodness and creativity of others. Through these social innovations, the outline of the new world emerges in vivid and brilliant colors, alive with creativity and diversity. An ever-evolving blueprint for a positive future is revealed in the countless acts of excellence and love now evolving our world.

We enter a period of lifelong learning while reaching out through our colleagues, organizations, and media to communicate the NewNews. We find that whatever age we are chronologically, we are very young from the point of view of our chosen work. Cocreators are all in the early stages of the new human archetype, gaining resources, skills, and know-how in the great task of repatterning and cocreating a world. As the larger system builds up its perturbations and instabilities, our infinitesimal positive steps tend increasingly to connect and converge.

Through this accelerated interaction of innovating elements, society appears to repattern itself — a dissipative structure moving to greater complexity. The change may seem to be a sudden quantum jump, but it is actually the fruit of the long, laborious, dedicated work of millions of souls, known and unknown, who like ourselves have been called from within to express their life purpose in service to the world. The larger metapattern joins us into a new whole, different from and far greater than the sum of our parts. The societal butterfly appears replete with greater freedom, consciousness, and synergistic order, glorious beyond the imagination of the individual.

To Take a Stand

The purpose of *Conscious Evolution: Awakening the Power of Our Social Potential* is to discover a peaceful passageway through the labyrinth of modern society, to carry us from here to there, to unearth a design of evolution for a gentle birth, and to formulate a spirit-motivated process of action to cooperate with the tendency in evolution for higher consciousness and greater freedom through more complex or synergistic order.

Is this plan possible? It depends on you and me.

When I visited Joan Holmes in her office in New York City during my vice-presidential campaign, she told me of the origins of the Hunger Project, which takes a stand for the sustainable end of world hunger.

"Who started this?" I asked.

"I did," she said. "I took a stand that there would be no more hunger."

I was amazed. At first she took the stand alone. Each of us at some point in our lives takes a stand alone. But the moment we do, we find we are surrounded by others who have also taken a stand. Even if our intention doesn't seem to have been fully realized, the collective impact of our choices is moving us forward in the right direction.

I take a stand for the gentle transition of humanity toward a future equal to our full potential. I join all others taking such a stand. Together we are a mighty force.

When asked what I choose to be the outcome of the book, my answer is that it serve the fulfillment of the plan.

"May Light and Love and Power restore the plan on Earth." That is my prayer.

AFTERWORD

A Call to Action

C *onscious Evolution: Awakening the Power of Our Social Potential* is a vision of our future to inspire us to activate our spiritual, social, and scientific/technological capacities. We are living at the precise shift point between devolution and evolution. Because there are so many people working toward the goal of "gentling the birth" to our next stage of evolution, I believe that the social potential movement is cresting right now.

We are fortunate to have so many social innovations to help us surf this very pivotal moment in history, but they are not connected. The most obvious next step in awakening the power of our social potential is to connect the golden innovations working toward higher consciousness, freedom, and order in every field and function, as mentioned in chapter 11. We also need to increase interconnectivity among groups of people already attracted to evolving together and cocreating a world in which we can do so.

The time has come to accelerate the synergy among all of us already attracted to evolving together. This is the call that conscious evolutionaries must make together now — a call for a more effective process of collaboration among the many projects, people, and innovations already moving in this direction, as exemplified by the Wheel of Cocreation and the SYNCON process.

This shared planetary purpose goes beyond any existing project or organization. Yet we must call for this new level of global collaboration to occur systematically and intentionally. It is our challenge to discover how to facilitate social synergy, the coming together of separate people and projects to make a new whole greater than the sum of its parts. This is nature's way. We can learn it, because we *are* nature evolving.

I suggest that you now take some time to contemplate your deepest heart's desire. Ask yourself these questions: "What is my intention? What I am called to do?"

As an example, here is my intention:

I intend to be a global voice to accelerate humanity's conscious evolution, to help catalyze the "global moon shot."

I intend to participate in the cocreation of a new evolutionary educational system to serve the community of pioneering souls to connect with one another worldwide to realize their potential as universal humans.

I dedicate all my teachings, movies, books, tapes, and 186 volumes of journals as a living legacy for this purpose.

Once you have identified your personal intention, take action toward it with courage and persistence. Through that action you'll be connected to the vast movement for positive change.

The Evolutionary Communion and Evolutionary Chakra Meditations

To accelerate our journey toward conscious evolution, it can be helpful to experience the Wheel of Cocreation spiritually, so that we can embody the whole story of creation within ourselves. Below are two meditations I have developed to facilitate that process.

The Evolutionary Communion: Embodying the Sacred Story of Creation

To help you activate and embody the impulse of evolution as alive in you in this very moment, I encourage you to read this meditation aloud as you remember the symbol of the Spiral and the Wheel. Create a sacred space by lighting candles and putting on beautiful music, and then begin reading.

We conscious evolutionaries represent a deep communion of pioneering souls, from every race, nation, and religion, who

experience within ourselves the emergence of a universal
human, a cocreator of new worlds.
Our crisis is the birth of a universal humanity.
Let us remember and embody our birth story, our sacred journey
*   of creation:*
Out of the mind of God
Out of the cosmic field
Out of no thing at all is arising everything that was, is, and will be.
The Evolutionary Spiral is unfolding —
The great flaring forth,
The formation of energy, matter, the billions upon billions of
*   galaxies,*
The trillions of planetary bodies, some of which may have life
*   comparable to our own.*

Now focus on our beautiful blue planet Earth:

Mother Earth is giving birth to life,
To animal life,
To human life,
And now to us, going around the next turn on the Spiral.

We place the crisis of our birth in the vast unfolding story of
*   creation.*
We feel the pain of Earth as the emergence of our birth.
We struggle to coordinate ourselves as one planetary body.
We feel the core of the Spiral as the universal love and intelligence
*   animating the whole process of creation within us,*
Incarnating within each of us as our own impulse to create, to
*   express, to give our unique gift more fully into the whole.*
In our atoms, molecules, and cells is encoded the whole story of
*   creation.*
We are the universe in person.

*We are entering our turn on the Spiral — the Wheel of
 Cocreation.*

*We reside at the center of the Wheel, where the core of the Spiral
 is awakening in our hearts.*

*We are in the presence of the global communion of pioneering
 souls, each of us animated from within by the same core of
 the Spiral, the universal intelligence of creation, connecting
 now in Spirit and in small groups to evolve ourselves and the
 world.*

*We invite this impulse of evolution within us to commune with
 the impulse within others, joining together with the universal
 impulse of creation empowering us all together.*

*Moved by the sacred core within us, we discover our unique
 callings. We reach out and offer our gifts into the whole
 process of cocreation.*

*The power that coordinates atoms, molecules, and cells is now
 coordinating us.*

We are becoming a cocreative, coevolving species.

*We enter the ecstasy of the planetary birthing experience healing
 ourselves as we love one another.*

*We bring these higher vibrations of energy downward into
 every chakra, infusing our higher mind, our voice, our
 vocation, our unconditional love, our emotions, our will, our
 generative organs, and our sense of security.*

*Within ourselves, we integrate what is rising within us with what
 is descending from beyond us.*

*We breathe all aspects of creation within ourselves. We are
 becoming whole beings, universal humans, imbued with
 the irresistible love and intelligence of the whole process of
 creation. We are the universe in person evolving.*

*I am alive at the dawn of our birth as a cocreative, universal
 species. For this I give thanks and am filled with gratitude
 and joy as I experience the reality of life ever evolving
 within myself.*

The Evolutionary Chakra Meditation: Incarnating the Core of the Spiral

This meditation, taken from my booklet *Evolutionary Communion*, can help you embody the core of the Spiral as your own impulse of creation. I have found that it can evolve every chakra of your being, reaching to the highest frequencies of your spirit, all the way through every cell in your body. It can be healing and regenerating whether it is done alone or with others.

Take a series of deep breaths. Visualize the universal Spiral of creation. Feel the core of the Spiral rising up from the mind of the cosmos, from the field of all possibilities. Now begin to bring that core upward into your own body-mind and embody the following meditation by reading it aloud:

I place my attention on the first chakra, the root center of physical experience located at the base of the spine. This base chakra symbolizes my own groundedness and security.

In that chakra, now, I place my attention on the great creating process of evolution itself. Out of the mind of the cosmos, out of the mind of God, there has arisen a force so great that it has expressed itself in matter, in life, in animal life, in human life; and now this mighty force of creation is entering into the transition of human life to a more universal humanity. My security and my groundedness are in that process of creation itself. I rest my security in the force of consciousness that is creating universes, worlds, and my own body-mind. With this, I feel the power of the process of creation entering into the base chakra with all the dynamism of the evolutionary consciousness of life itself lifting, sustaining, and entering my body as my security. I have complete and utter trust in this process of creation.

I breathe that now into the second chakra, of the generative organs. As I breathe the mighty force of creation in, I experience the transition of my cellular DNA — from its phase of degeneration to its phase of regeneration, from its phase of procreation to its phase of cocreation. I breathe the mighty process of creation into my generative organs and awaken the potency of life as it begins to move into its cocreative conscious evolutionary phase within me. I place this code within my own DNA, this thought code that I am now a regenerating being. My body is responsive to my intention to create, as long as that power of creativity is alive in me. I feel the shift at the cellular level.

I return to Source, to the mind of God, and I breathe up through the whole process of creation, through the formation of universe, energy, matter, Earth, life, human life, and universal human life ever-evolving, upward through the first chakra of my security and the second chakra of my regeneration. I feel every cell awakening to its untapped potential to shift from the phase of Homo sapiens, *degenerating, into* Homo universalis, *regenerating as an expression of the continuity of life itself.*

Continuing to breathe all the way through the billions of years, up through the first chakra and the generative organs, I now breathe into the third chakra of the will and power, located just below the navel. In this chakra, I place my will as an individual human within the will and power of the process of creation itself, feeling the mighty force that has arisen to ever-greater consciousness and freedom, through ever-more-complex order for billions and billions of years, now arising within me.

I know that purpose is my purpose, that will is my will. I have no other will but that — to join my individual will with the will of

*the process of creation to transcend its own limits, to create beings
ever more conscious of the processes that are creating us. With
that, my will becomes the mighty will of the force of creation
itself.*

*Then I continue and breathe with the flow of creation arising
from the mind of God, the ever-present origin, into the rising
power of creation, up through the base chakra, up through the
generative organs, up through my will — now at one with the
will of the process of creation.*

*I move upward into my emotions, into all my feelings: my
anxieties, my concerns, my empathy, my sympathy, my love,
my tensions. I release them into this process whose momentum
is so great that all my emotions are oriented upward, aligned
with the motivational power and force of creation itself. All my
feelings are being guided toward the evolution of life itself. In
the face of that mighty process of creation, my mal-aligned
emotions are magnetized, reoriented, moving me into the next
chakra, which is my heart.*

*I have two parts within the heart chakra. Within the lower heart
is unconditional love. Breathing up through the billions of years
of creation, through the base chakra, through the generative
organs, the will, and the emotions, I breathe now into the
experience of unconditional love.*

*The essence, the source, the intrinsic beingness of the process of
creation is love itself — not love of someone or about something,
but love itself. In that lower heart, I open up to love: the love
of God, the love of the process, the love of creation, and the
immense, magnificent, magnanimous evolutionary love that*

is creating all existence. In that love I place my personal love. I dwell in love with all those who I can remember in my life. I experience loving them and sending them this love of the whole process of creation; I am feeling the process of creation coming alive, becoming conscious within them. I join with them in my heart, the love of all creation now evolving humanity.

In the experience of empathy for all that is, we are lifting up out of our separation into divine union. The illusion of separation is dissolving.

Going through all the billions of years again, up through all the chakras, I come to the upper heart, where I find my vocation — my gift of love into the world. This vocation is not only personal; it is also the expression of divine intent, localized in me, in a pure gift of love of this unique aspect of the creation. My vocation now rides on the power and the presence and the motivational process of universal creation itself. It is lifted up by that process of creation, rising up into its divine expression in the world, spreading itself everywhere.

This leads me up into the throat chakra. In my throat is the rising up of the word. When I speak the word it embodies and resonates with the power and presence of creation itself. In the beginning is the word. Every word spoken reflects the resonance, and expresses the resonance, of the whole process of creation flowing through me. I speak my word as that now.

I rise up from there into the Third Eye. I open up to the higher mind, the intuitive mind, the enlightened mind that knows and guides the whole process of creation. My mental mind is at rest and cradled in the higher mind, coming on only when needed,

*as the higher mind begins to infuse my own mentality with its
illumination and genius of direct knowing.*

*Once again I breathe up through all the billions of years of
creation. I expand my breath to include the entire process of
universal creation arising upward from Earth life into my life,
evolving me with every breath I take.*

*The mighty impulse of evolution continues upward through the
top of my head, the crown chakra rising, rising, connecting me
with higher dimensions and frequencies of reality, with masters,
avatars, beings coming from other planetary wombs, within the
living universe without end.*

*Now I bring these higher vibrations of energy downward into
every chakra, infusing my higher mind, my voice, my vocation,
my unconditional love, my emotions, my will, my generative
organs, and sense of security. I integrate within myself what is
rising within me with what is descending from beyond me.*

*I breathe all aspects of creation within myself. I am becoming
a whole being, a universal human, imbued with the irresistible
love and intelligence of the whole process of creation. I am the
universe in person evolving. I am alive at the dawn of our birth
as a cocreative, universal species. For this I give thanks and am
filled with gratitude and joy as I experience the reality of life
ever evolving within me.*

Endnotes

Acknowledgments

1. Sidney Lanier, *The Sovereign Person: A Soul's Call to Conscious Evolution* (Santa Barbara, CA: Foundation for Conscious Evolution, 2010).

Chapter One. The Awakening of Humanity

1. Jonas Salk, *Anatomy of Reality: Merging of Intuition and Reason* (New York: Columbia University Press, 1983).
2. Eric Chaisson, *The Life Era: Cosmic Selection and Conscious Evolution* (New York: W. W. Norton and Co., 1989).
3. Eric Chaisson, "Our Cosmic Heritage," *ZYGON* 23, no. 4 (December 1988).
4. Paul Hawken, *Blessed Unrest: How the Largest Movement in the World Came into Being and Why No One Saw It Coming* (New York: Viking Penguin, 2007).
5. Ferris Jabr, "How Does a Caterpillar Turn into a Butterfly?" *Scientific American*, August 10, 2012, www.scientificamerican.com/article.cfm?id=caterpillar -butterfly-metamorphosis-explainer.
6. Duane Elgin with Coleen LeDrew, *Global Consciousness Change: Indicators of an Emerging Paradigm*, http://duaneelgin.com/global-consciousness-change -emerging-paradigm (accessed May 22, 2014). Collaborating organizations: the Fetzer Institute, the Institute of Noetic Sciences, the Brande Foundation, the California Institute of Integral Studies, the State of the World Forum (Millennium Project, 1997).

7. Paul H. Ray, *The Integral Culture Survey: A Study of Transformational Values in America* (Research Report 96-A, Institute of Noetic Sciences in partnership with the Fetzer Institute, 1996).

8. Paul H. Ray, *The Potential for a New, Emerging Culture in the U.S.: Report on the 2008 American Values Survey*, chapter 2, "The Cultural Creatives" (Boise, ID: Wisdom University, 2008), www.wisdomuniversity.org/CCsReport2008 SurveyV3.pdf (accessed October 3, 2014).

9. Marilyn Ferguson, *The Aquarian Conspiracy: Personal and Social Transformation in Our Time* (New York: G. P. Putnam's Sons, new edition, 1987).

10. Teilhard de Chardin, *The Phenomenon of Man* (New York: Harper & Row, 1975).

11. Abraham H. Maslow, *Toward a Psychology of Being*. 2nd ed. (New York: Van Nostrand Reinhold, 1982); Abraham H. Maslow, *The Further Reaches of Human Nature* (New York: Penguin/Arkana, 1993); Viktor Frankl, *Man's Search for Meaning* (New York: Washington Square Press, 1985); and Robert Assagioli, *Psychosynthesis: A Manual of Principles and Techniques* (New York: Viking Press, 1971).

Chapter Two. Discovering the Importance of the New Story

1. Giovanni Pico della Mirandola, *Oration on the Dignity of Man* (New York: Bobbs-Merrill, 1940).

Chapter Three. The Evolutionary Spiral

1. Barbara Marx Hubbard, *The Evolutionary Journey: A Personal Guide to a Positive Future* (San Francisco: Evolutionary Press, 1982).

2. Stanislav Grof, *The Adventure of Self-Discovery: Dimensions of Consciousness and New Perspectives in Psychotherapy and Inner Exploration* (Albany, NY: State University of New York Press, 1988).

3. Daniel C. Matt, *God and the Big Bang: Discovering the Harmony between Science and Spirituality* (Woodstock, VT: Jewish Lights Publishing, 1996).

4. Brian Swimme and Thomas Berry, *The Universe Story: From the Primordial Flaring Forth to the Ecozoic Era* (San Francisco: HarperCollins, 1992).

5. Krafft A. Ehricke, "Extraterrestrial Imperative," *Bulletin of the Atomic Scientists*, November 1971.

6. Riane Eisler, *The Chalice and the Blade* (San Francisco: HarperSanFrancisco, 1987).

7. Michael Grosso, *Frontiers of the Soul* (Wheaton, IL: Quest Books, 1992).

8. Gregory Stock, *Metaman: The Merging of Humans and Machines into a Global Superorganism* (New York: Simon & Schuster, 1993).

9. Duane Elgin, *Awakening Earth: Exploring the Evolution of Human Culture and Consciousness* (New York: William Morrow and Company, 1993).

Chapter Four. Our Crisis Is a Birth

1. Buckminster Fuller, *Operating Manual for Spaceship Earth* (New York: Penguin, 1991).
2. Eric Chaisson, *The Life Era: Cosmic Selection and Conscious Evolution* (New York: W. W. Norton and Co., 1989).
3. John Randolph Price, *The Planetary Commission* (Austin, TX: Quartus Foundation for Spiritual Research, 1984).
4. Peter Russell, *The Global Brain Awakens: Our Next Evolutionary Leap* (Palo Alto, CA: Global Brain, 1995).
5. United Nations, Department of Economic and Social Affairs, Population Division, "World Population Prospects: The 2012 Revision" (press release), June 13, 2013.
6. Rupert Sheldrake, *A New Science of Life: The Hypothesis of Formative Causation* (Los Angeles: J. P. Tarcher, 1981).
7. Peter Russell, *The White Hole in Time: Our Future Evolution and the Meaning of Now* (San Francisco: HarperSanFrancisco, 1992).
8. Jan Smuts, *Holism and Evolution* (Westport, CT: Greenwood Press, 1973).
9. Pierre Teilhard de Chardin, *The Phenomenon of Man* (New York: HarperCollins, 1975).
10. David B. Ellis, *Creating Your Future: A Guide to Long-Range Visioning* (New York: Houghton Mifflin, 1998).
11. Kenneth Cox, "A Futurist Perspective for Space," PowerPoint presentation, 2001, http://settlement.arc.nasa.gov/SpaceFuturist.pdf (accessed October 3, 2014).

Chapter Five. Conscious Evolution

1. Eric Chaisson, "Our Cosmic Heritage," *ZYGON* 23, no. 4 (December 1988).
2. Beatrice Bruteau, "Symbiotic Cosmos," *The Roll: Newsletter of the Schola Contemplationis*, December 1993.
3. Timothy Leary, *Info-Psychology (A Re-Vision of Exo-Psychology): A Manual on the Use of the Human Nervous System According to the Instructions of the Manufacturers* (Las Vegas: New Falcon Press, 1989).
4. Bruce Lipton, *The Biology of Belief: Unleashing the Power of Consciousness, Matter, & Miracles* (Carlsbad, CA: Hay House, 2007).
5. Alfred Korzybski, *Science and Sanity: Introduction to Non-Aristotelian Systems and General Semantics* (Lakeville, CT: International Non-Aristotelian Library Publishing Co., 1958).

Chapter Six. Exploring the Meaning of Conscious Evolution

1. Richard Elliott Friedman, *The Disappearance of God: A Divine Mystery* (New York: Little, Brown and Co., 1995).

2. Theodore B. Roszak, *The Voice of the Earth* (New York: Simon & Schuster, 1992).

3. Erich Jantsch, *Design for Evolution: Self-Organization and Planning in the Life of Human Systems* (New York: George Braziller, 1975).

4. Hazel Henderson, *Building a Win-Win World: Life Beyond Global Economics* (San Francisco: Barrett-Koehler Publishers, 1996); Elisabet Sahtouris, "The Biology of Globalization," *Perspectives on Business and Global Change* 2, no. 3 (September 1997), www.worldbusiness.org/wp-content/uploads/2013/07/pro997es.pdf (accessed October 3, 2014).

5. Jerome Clayton Glenn, *Future Mind: Artificial Intelligence — Merging the Mystical and the Technological in the 21st Century* (Washington, DC: Acropolis Books, 1989).

6. Nassim Haramein, conversation with author, 2007.

Chapter Seven. The Fabric of Civilization

1. Richard Dawkins, *The Selfish Gene*, 30th anniv. ed. (New York: Oxford University Press, 2006).

2. Howard Bloom, *The Lucifer Principle: A Scientific Expedition into the Forces of History* (New York: Atlantic Monthly Press, 1995).

3. Daniel Jonah Goldhagen, *Hitler's Willing Executioners: Ordinary Germans and the Holocaust* (New York: Vintage Books/Random House, 1997).

4. Bloom, *The Lucifer Principle*.

5. John Shelby Spong, *Liberating the Gospels* (New York: HarperCollins, 1996).

6. Ilia Delio, *The Emergent Christ: Exploring the Meaning of Catholic in an Evolutionary Universe* (Maryknoll, NY: Orbis Books, 2011); and Ilia Delio, *Christ in Evolution* (Maryknoll, NY: Orbis Books, 2008).

7. Theodore B. Roszak, *The Voice of the Earth* (New York: Simon & Schuster, 1992).

8. Ken Wilber, *A Brief History of Everything* (Boston and London: Shambhala, 1996).

9. Arthur Schlesinger, *The Disuniting of America: Reflections on a Multicultural Society* (New York: Norton, 1993).

10. Ervin Laszlo, *The Chaos Point 2012 and Beyond: Appointment with Destiny* (Charlottesville, VA: Hampton Roads, 2012).

11. Paul Hawken, *The Ecology of Commerce: A Declaration of Sustainability* (New York: HarperBusiness, 1993).

12. George Soros, "The Capitalist Threat," *Atlantic Monthly*, February 1997.

13. Alfred Korzybski, *Science and Sanity: Introduction to Non-Aristotelian Systems and General Semantics* (Lakeville, CT: International Non-Aristotelian Library Publishing Co., 1958).

14. David L. Cooperrider, *Appreciative Management and Leadership: The Power of Positive Thinking and Action in Organizations* (San Francisco: Jossey-Bass, 1990).

Chapter Eight. Embracing Conscious Evolution

1. Mihaly Csikszentmihalyi, *Flow: The Psychology of Optimal Experience* (New York: HarperCollins, 2008).

2. John Geirland, "Go with the Flow," *Wired*, September 1996, http://archive .wired.com/wired/archive/4.09/czik_pr.html.

3. Sidney Lanier, *The Sovereign Person: A Soul's Call to Conscious Evolution* (Santa Barbara, CA: Foundation for Conscious Evolution, 2010).

4. Professor A. Harris Stone, personal correspondence with author, 1997.

5. Deepak Chopra, *The Seven Spiritual Laws of Success: A Practical Guide to the Fulfillment of Your Dreams* (San Rafael, CA: Amber-Allen/New World Library, 1994).

Chapter Nine. From the Human Potential to the Social Potential Movement

1. M. Mitchell Waldrop, "The Trillion-Dollar Vision of Dee Hock," *Fast Company*, October/November 1996, www.fastcompany.com/27333/trillion-dollar-vision -dee-hock.

2. Ilya Prigogine, "A Chemist Told How Life Could Defy Physics Laws," *New York Times*, October 12, 1977.

3. Marilyn Ferguson, *The Aquarian Conspiracy: Personal and Social Transformation in Our Time* (New York: Jeremy Tarcher/Putnam, 1987).

Chapter Ten. Testing the Waters

1. David L. Cooperrider, "Appreciative Inquiry: A Constructive Approach to Organizational Development and Change," *Research in Organizational Change and Development*, vol. I (Greenwich, CT: J.A.I. Press, 1987).

2. Alvin Toffler, *Future Shock* (New York: Random House, 1984); and Alvin Toffler, *The Third Wave* (New York: Bantam, 1991).

3. Carolyn Anderson with Katharine Roske, *The Co-Creator's Handbook: An Experiential Guide for Discovering Your Life's Purpose and Building a Co-Creative Society* (Penn Valley, CA: Global Family, 2001).

4. Paul Ray, PhD, quoted in "Same Planet, Different Worlds: How Cultural Creatives Are Transcending Alienation and Isolation to Bring Forward the Practical Wisdom of Conscious Living — An Interview with Social Scientist Paul Ray, PhD," *Kindred*, September 15, 2013, www.kindredcommunity .com/2013/09/same-planet-different-worlds-how-cultural-creatives-are -bringing-forward-the-practical-wisdom-of-conscious-living.

Chapter Eleven. A Spirit-Motivated Process of Action for the Twenty-First Century

1. David L. Cooperrider, "Appreciative Inquiry: A Constructive Approach to Organizational Development and Change," *Research in Organizational Change and Development*, vol. I (Greenwich, CT: J.A.I. Press, 1987).

2. C. Otto Scharmer, *Theory U: Leading from the Future as It Emerges* (San Francisco: Berrett-Koehler, 2009); Peter Senge, C. Otto Scharmer, Joseph Jaworski, and Betty Sue Flowers, *Presence: An Exploration of Profound Change in People, Organizations, and Society* (New York: Crown Business, 2005).

3. Justin Rosenstein, "Do Great Things — Your Role in the Human Project," Wisdom 2.0 speech, 2013, www.youtube.com/watch?v=mivoSvYusAU.

4. Justin Rosenstein, email correspondence with author, 2013.

5. Bharat Mitra, email correspondence with author, 2014.

6. Eleanor LeCain, with an introduction by His Holiness the Dalai Lama, *Breakthrough Solutions: How to Improve Your Life and Change the World by Building on What Works* (Washington, DC: New Way Press, 2011).

7. David L. Cooperrider, "Appreciative Inquiry: A Constructive Approach to Organizational Development and Change," *Research in Organizational Change and Development*, vol. I (Greenwich, CT: J.A.I. Press, 1987).

8. The Millennium Project, "About Us," n.d., www.millennium-project.org /overview.html (accessed October 3, 2014).

9. LeCain, *Breakthrough Solutions*.

10. Corinne McLaughlin and Gordon Davidson, *The Practical Visionary: A New World Guide to Spiritual and Social Change* (Unity Village, MO: Unity House, 2010). McLaughlin has also correlated each of the Wheel's twelve sectors with an astrological sign and created a community ritual and meditation using the Wheel; see "Inspiring Solutions on the Wheel of Cocreation," Center for Visionary Leadership, n.d., www.visionarylead.org/articles/wheel_cocreation.htm (accessed October 3, 2014).

Chapter Twelve. A Pattern of Transformation Revealed

1. Mihaly Csikszentmihalyi, *The Evolving Self: A Psychology for the Third Millennium* (New York: HarperCollins, 1993).

2. Carl Jung, *Synchronicity: An Acausal Connecting Principle* (Princeton, NJ: Princeton University Press, 1969).

3. Erich Jantsch, *Design for Evolution: Self-Organization and Planning in the Life of Human Systems* (New York: George Braziller, 1975).

Chapter Thirteen. The NewNews

1. David B. Ellis and Stan Lankowitz, *Creating Your Future: A Guide to Long Range Visioning* (Rapid City, SD: Breakthrough Enterprises, 1997); and Dave Ellis and Stan Lankowitz, *Human Being: A Manual for Happiness, Health, Love, and Wealth* (Rapid City, SD: Breakthrough Enterprises, 1997).
2. James Redfield, *The Tenth Insight* (New York: Warner Books, 1996); and James Redfield, *The Celestine Vision* (New York: Warner Books, 1997).

Chapter Fourteen. Education for Conscious Evolution

1. Ralph Abraham, *Chaos, Gaia, Eros* (San Francisco: HarperSanFrancisco, 1994).
2. Gregory Bateson, *Mind and Nature: A Necessary Unity* (New York: Bantam, 1979).
3. Paul Taylor, email correspondence with author, 2014.
4. Michael Grosso, *The Millennium Myth: Love and Death at the End of Time* (Wheaton, IL: Quest Books, 1995).
5. Richard Maurice Bucke, MD, *Cosmic Consciousness: A Classic Investigation of the Development of Man's Mystic Relationship to the Infinite* (New York: E. P. Dutton, 1969).
6. O. W. Markley, "Human Consciousness in Transformation," *Evolution and Consciousness: Human Systems in Transition*, ed. Erich Jantsch and Conrad H. Waddington (Reading, MA: Addison-Wesley, 1976).
7. Hazel Henderson, *The Politics of the Solar Age* (Garden City, NY: Anchor/Doubleday, 1981).
8. Eric K. Drexler, *The Engines of Creation: The Coming Era of Nanotechnology* (New York: Anchor/Doubleday, 1986).

Chapter Fifteen. The Great Awakening

1. Ken Carey, *The Third Millennium: Living in the Posthistoric World* (San Francisco: HarperSanFrancisco, 1995).
2. Teilhard de Chardin, *The Future of Man* (New York: HarperCollins, 1959).
3. Neale Donald Walsch, *The Mother of Invention: The Legacy of Barbara Marx Hubbard and the Future of YOU* (Carlsbad, CA: Hay House, 2011).

Chapter Sixteen. The Cocreative Society Revealed

1. Gary Zukav, *The Seat of the Soul* (New York: Simon & Schuster, 1990).
2. Ervin Laszlo, *The Whispering Pond: A Personal Guide to the Emerging Vision of Science* (Rockport, MA: Element, 1996).

3. Michael Murphy, *The Future of the Body: Explorations into the Further Evolution of Human Nature* (Los Angeles: Jeremy P. Tarcher, 1992).

4. Jerome Clayton Glenn, *Future Mind: Artificial Intelligence — Merging the Mystical and the Technological in the 21st Century* (Washington, DC: Acropolis Books, 1989).

5. Deepak Chopra, *Ageless Body, Timeless Mind* (New York: Random House, 1993).

6. Eric Drexler, *Engines of Creation: The Coming Era of Nanotechnology* (New York: Anchor/Doubleday, 1986).

7. Ted Chu, PhD, *Human Purpose and Transhuman Potential* (San Rafael, CA: Origin Press, 2014), 381.

8. Peter H. Diamandis and Steven Kotler, *Abundance: The Future Is Better Than You Think* (New York: Free Press, 2012).

9. Barbara Marx Hubbard, *The Evolutionary Journey: A Personal Guide to a Positive Future* (San Francisco: Evolutionary Press, 1982), 93–94.

About the Foundation
for Conscious Evolution

The Foundation for Conscious Evolution is a nonprofit educational institution cofounded in 1993 by Barbara Marx Hubbard and Sidney Lanier to accelerate conscious evolution. Its mission is to educate, communicate, and nurture humanity's potential for self- and social evolution. An awakened humanity in harmony with nature for the highest good of all life is its ultimate goal.

The foundation's initiatives offer a context and a container for connecting and empowering the global movements for positive change, making the efforts of this movement visible to engender greater coherence and synergy. By connecting and communicating what's working, positive, and innovative, the Foundation for Conscious Evolution is helping to accelerate evolution, to build a new path — a "golden bridge" — to the next stage of human emergence.

Please visit the foundation's website for a comprehensive study of the works of Barbara Marx Hubbard and the resources, initiatives, programs, and evolutionary educational offerings of the Foundation for Conscious Evolution: www.Evolve.org.

About the Author

Barbara Marx Hubbard is a noted futurist, evolutionary thought leader, social innovator, public speaker, and the author of eight books. She is president of the Foundation for Conscious Evolution and cofounder of many organizations, including the World Future Society and the Association for Global New Thought. She is the producer and narrator of the award-winning documentary series *Humanity Ascending: A New Way through Together*. She partnered with The Shift Network to launch the Birth 2012 movement on December 22, 2012. Through The Shift Network, she teaches a variety of courses on the theme of conscious evolution to thousands of students.

In 1984 her name was placed in nomination for the vice presidency of the United States on the Democratic ticket. She called for an Office for the Future and a Peace Room in the White House to scan for, map, connect, and communicate what is working in the world. As cofounder of the Committee for the Future in Washington, DC, in the 1970s, she developed the Theater for the Future and the SYNCON (SYNergistic CONvergence) process, bringing opposing groups together for win-win solutions in twenty-five conferences, as well as in several Soviet-American Citizen Summits during the Cold War. She produced a fourteen-part television series, *Potentials*, interviewing some of our greatest futurists, including Buckminster Fuller, Norman Cousins, Gene Roddenberry, Willis Harmon, Marilyn Ferguson, and others.

She is a fellow of the Club of Budapest and of the Laszlo New-Paradigm Leadership Center. She established the first Chair in Conscious Evolution at Wisdom University Graduate School and is a member of many progressive groups, including the Evolutionary Leaders Group, the Transformational Leadership Council, and the Association for Global New Thought.

She has been the recipient of many awards including the first Peacebuilder Award from the Peace Alliance in Washington, DC. Her books include *The Hunger of Eve*, *The Evolutionary Journey*, *The Revelation*, *Emergence*, *The 52 Codes for Conscious Self Evolution*, *Conscious Evolution*, *Birth 2012 and Beyond*, and *Evolutionary Testament: The Promise Will Be Kept — Gospels, Acts, and Epistles from an Evolutionary Perspective*.

She graduated cum laude from Bryn Mawr College with a BA in political science. She also studied at La Sorbonne and L'École des Sciences Politiques in Paris. She has five children and eight grandchildren and lives in Santa Barbara, California.

For more information on Barbara's work, projects, meditations, and courses, go to www.Evolve.org.

NEW WORLD LIBRARY is dedicated to publishing books and other media that inspire and challenge us to improve the quality of our lives and the world.

We are a socially and environmentally aware company. We recognize that we have an ethical responsibility to our customers, our staff members, and our planet.

We serve our customers by creating the finest publications possible on personal growth, creativity, spirituality, wellness, and other areas of emerging importance. We serve New World Library employees with generous benefits, significant profit sharing, and constant encouragement to pursue their most expansive dreams.

As a member of the Green Press Initiative, we print an increasing number of books with soy-based ink on 100 percent postconsumer-waste recycled paper. Also, we power our offices with solar energy and contribute to non-profit organizations working to make the world a better place for us all.

Our products are available in bookstores everywhere.

www.newworldlibrary.com

At NewWorldLibrary.com you can download our catalog,
subscribe to our e-newsletter, read our blog,
and link to authors' websites, videos, and podcasts.

Find us on Facebook, follow us on Twitter, and watch us on YouTube.

Send your questions and comments our way!
You make it possible for us to do what we love to do.

Phone: 415-884-2100 or 800-972-6657
Catalog requests: Ext. 10 | Orders: Ext. 52 | Fax: 415-884-2199
escort@newworldlibrary.com

NEW WORLD LIBRARY
publishing books that change lives   14 Pamaron Way, Novato, CA 94949